The Soul of the Wolf

The Soul

of the Wolf

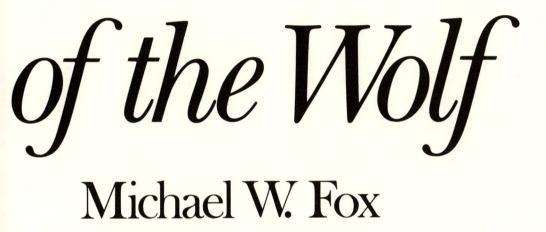

Michael W. Fox

Lyons & Burford, Publishers

Printed in the United States of America

10 9 8 7 6 5 4 3

LIBRARY OF CONGRESS CATALOGING-IN-PUBLICATION DATA
Fox, Michael W.,   1937-
    The soul of the wolf / Michael W. Fox.
        p.   cm.
    Originally published: Boston: Little, Brown, c1980. With new foreword.
    Includes bibliographical references.
    ISBN 1-55821-150-0
    1. Wolves.   2. Wolves—Behavior.   3. Human-animal relationships.
I. Title.
[QL737.C22F693   1992]   599.74′442—dc20   92-13374
                                                        CIP

Unless otherwise noted, photographs are by Michael W. Fox.

Foreword to the 1992 Edition

Much has happened to wolves and other wild creatures of this world since *The Soul of the Wolf* was first published over a decade ago. The persecution of wolves and all wild predators of the land, air, and sea continues to intensify. Soon there may be only captive-bred wolves in zoos and wildlife parks, along with dwindling numbers left in the wild. They may be well cared for and receive good veterinary and scientific attention to ensure continuation of these chosen species—remnants of a once vibrant, beautiful, and beneficient Earth. Mother of us all.

Now the Earth is beginning to fail us because we have failed her. We have failed from a Christian perspective (according to the second Genesis story of the Creation), "to dress and to keep" the garden of divine conception. Had we followed centuries ago the teachings of St. Francis of Assisi, who called the feared wolf of Gubbio his "little brother," and who enjoined all peoples to have respect and reverence for all creatures, the Earth would surely not be failing us today.

To be able to see wolves and other wild creatures only under captive conditions or "protective custody" in the future will mean the end of the wild. These animal survivors will lead impoverished lives under such artificial conditions, and may experience the stress and distress of an anomolous existence. So too may our descendants feel an emptiness and an unbearable sadness for never knowing, except from films, holograms, and books what the world of the First Creation was really like before it was transformed into a bioindustrialized wasteland.

I am grateful to my publishers for reissuing this book because I feel that it can help people have greater respect and reverence for wolves through an objective understanding and a sympathetic concern for their current plight. Concern for wolves or any creature is a first step into the boundless circle of compassion for all of Earth's creations. If we begin to see the world through the eyes of the wolf (and, from the perspective of my Lummi Indian friends and teachers, Kenny Cooper and Jewell "Praying Wolf" James, in a *sacred* or *shamanic* way), then the accelerating extinction of wolves, other endangered species, and their natural habitats might slow down* sufficiently so that some parts of the First Creation might be protected, restored, and conserved for all time.

Michael W. Fox
Washington, D.C.
Spring Equinox 1991

*Many steps to accomplish this, such as eating less meat, supporting wildlife protective legislation, and habitat preservation have been detailed in my book *You Can Save the Animals: 50 Things To Do Right Now.* New York: St. Martin's Press. 1991.

"Life outside a person is an extension of the life within him. This compells him to be part of it and accept responsibility for all creatures great and small. Life becomes harder when we live for others, but it also becomes richer and happier."

—Albert Schweitzer

Acknowledgments

I wish to thank all those people who have helped me in so many ways, not only in my wolf research, but also in bringing together the diverse aspects of the wolf — from its behavior and ecology to the politics and ethics at the wolf-man interface. My thanks go to Professors Tom Sandel, Viktor Hemburger, Owen Sexton, and Barry Commoner of Washington University, St. Louis, and to Carol and Marlin Perkins, Bruce and Cynthia Pitzinger, and all my friends and colleagues of the Wild Canid Survival and Research Center, St. Louis. Thanks also to other "wolf people," of whom there are many, especially Karlyn Atkinson Berg, John Harris, Drs. Erick Klinghammer, Dave Mech, Durward Allen, Konrad Lorenz, and Erik Zimen, and to former students, particularly Jim Cohen, Stewart Halperin, and Randy Lockwood: a diverse pack indeed.

As for my acknowledgment to my other friends and "colleagues" — the wolves — this book is their testimony and respectful tribute.

M. W. Fox

Contents

The Soul of the Wolf

Man is only fully alive when he is aware of his existence, and being deeply aware of one's existence is to be religious. A wolf is fully aware within the limits of its own being, no less than we are in relation to our own limits, and thus the wolf's existence, and that of any sentient being, should hold no less religious significance than life to man himself.

Introduction:
Lessons from the Wolf

This book is not a scientific treatise on wolf behavior and ecology (although short, informative "capsule" statements are included in the Appendix), nor is it another account of someone living in the wilderness with wild, or tame, hand-raised wolves. There are plenty of books along these lines, and children's books too, ranging from the factual to the extremes of fiction; I have written such myself. What this book offers is more than insights into the nature of wolves. It goes beyond the surface nature of both men and wolves, shattering the arbitrary, if not illusory, barriers between animal and man to explore the common ground within the essence of life that is shared by all sentient beings. Any life form could be such a key to heightened awareness of this "common ground" of kinship for mankind. It so happened that through and for me, the wolf be-

An adult wolf captured in a reflective mood by wildlife photographer Scott Barry.

came both mirror and teacher. These lessons from the wolf may not only help foster a reverence for all life within which lies our salvation from self-destruction, since our wholeness is dependent upon a healthy and whole earth, but our consummate fulfillment also as stewards of planet Earth; as cocreators working in sympathetic resonance with nature, which, until now, we have attempted to exploit, dominate, and subdue. But in so doing, we demean and ultimately threaten our own survival. Man and wolf are not only of one earth, but they are also of one essence. The wolf is an endangered species today, thanks to man; and mankind, through his own actions in ignorance, is no less endangered.

The wolf is a complex symbol, an archetype of many attributes good and bad that most human cultures have projected upon it since the beginning of recorded history. Today, science is coming to its rescue by destroying many myths about the wolf's vicious and blood-lusting nature, as well as by justifying its protection and conservation since the wolf plays a vital role in the balance of nature in its wilderness habitat. Those who have studied its family life see how close the wolf is to man in many ways and use this as evidence to favor its conservation. The same approach is used to justify the conservation of whales, dolphins, and the like — who, having complex brains like ours, should also be conserved since they are most like us, just as the wolves, socially, are more kin to us than perhaps our closest primate relatives.

But this book is not another conservationist plea to save the wolf — it is more a description of what I have learned from wolves: simply, lessons from the wolf. For me, it is also a celebration of life through understanding, through coming to know another species and, in essence, breaking through the alienating and artificial barrier between man and animal. Perhaps the only difference between man and animal is this very book, in that I have a way of communicating, of sharing my experiences and ideas, that no wolf has, except indirectly through me or some other human being who is attuned to it.

When you finish this book, you will know more about wolves and about yourself, and also perhaps will have gained some insights into human nature, into things of nature as a whole. The lessons from the wolf have opened my mind to a new, but very ancient reality — kinship with all life. I hope the wolf, through me, can do this for you also, and more, for you and I are as much responsible for the future of wolves as we are for our children and for all creatures of this earth.

Wolf Eyes

Although we perceive the outer, physical world with our eyes, we can also touch and sense something of the inner world of another through eye contact. This avenue into the inner being of another is not a mystical illusion but a very real key to communion. Emotions, fleeting reactions, and even intentions are reflected in subtle changes in the size of the pupils and in the movements of the muscles that control the eyes. In social contexts, the demeanor or "situational personality" of an individual is revealed in the eyes, whether the individual be a chimpanzee, a wolf, or a man. Other animals, those most "highly" or, more correctly, most *continuously* evolved, possess very similar eye reactions. This is especially evident in the more social and gregarious mammals, such as dogs and horses, and is a major channel and potential for communication between different species.

As in man, so in the wolf: a direct stare is a threat; looking down and away is a submissive or friendly signal; and a wide "innocent" gaze, an infantile open face, is associated with playful intentions. Changes in pupil size in both man and wolf correlate with changes in emotion — pleasure, pain, fear, and anger.

The wolf's eyes glow in the dark; there is a light-reflecting layer called the *tapetum lucidum* that may facilitate night vision. A carnivore's eyes are also usually extremely sensitive to movements, while color perception and visual acuity may be inferior to man's. The use — conscious and unconscious — of the eyes in social contexts, however, is virtually identical in man and wolf. This fact greatly facilitates communication across the species barrier between animal and man.

Rarely will one make direct eye contact with a wolf, wild or captive, unless the intention is to threaten (and possibly attack), or to engage in play. More usually, the wolf elusively avoids eye contact, but in a Mona Lisa way. You always know that the wolf is following you with its eyes whenever you are in its vicinity. When you make eye contact it may look away submissively, or even close its eyes in a relaxed catlike fashion (not ignoring you but displaying simply that it is at ease in your presence). Some wolves, like the big cats at the zoo, will instead look right through you as though you did not exist! This aloof gaze of passive indifference is an example of how the control of eye contact is an indicator of status and a regulator of social distance. The more submissive, dependent, or fearful wolf or human being makes more eye contact than does one who is more self-assured and of high status.

These reactions of making, breaking, and regulating eye contact are clear indices of social rank and personality. A steady, confident, and unvarying gaze speaks silent volumes of the potential energy, emotional balance, and latent or actual awareness of an individual — wolf or man.

Both wolf and man have the eyes set in front of the face, a mark of the hunter who searches and penetrates his visual field for prey. (For man, this frontal orientation of the eyes is also essential for visual regulation of manual dexterity, manipulative abilities being greatly limited if the eyes were placed more to the sides of the head.) This is distinct from the wide-set eyes of prey species, who have an almost 360-degree all-round vision essential for scanning and detecting the presence of a stalking predator.

Two people, at close proximity, will often close their eyes and then touch. Eye closure in such contexts may be associated with pleasure, especially when the two embrace. Similarly, a wolf will close its eyes in pleasure when it is being groomed by a companion. With one of my wolves, eye contact with me at very close proximity is often followed by the animal's reaching out and touching me lightly on the cheek with a forepaw. The wolf, with

Direct eye contact by a superior wolf is a "put down" to a subordinate, who presents a submission "grin" and then avoids eye contact quickly.

A wolf enjoys rolling in the scent of a deer.

Rarely will a wolf look you (or the camera) straight on: its natural social deference in avoiding eye contact is often misinterpreted by man as a sign of sly cunning and untrustworthiness.

eyes closed, then leans forward and presses her forehead against mine for several seconds, a simple "embrace" of body against body. Also, wolves, like dogs, will rear up and embrace each other with their forelimbs in a pattern identical to man.

This, to me, is communion. Nothing is specifically communicated (friendly or aggressive intentions or expectations) but rather the animal simply expresses an unconditional trust and acceptance of me. Soon after, however, the wolf rolls over onto one side, elevates her uppermost hindleg, and, looking away with half-closed eyes, breaks passive communion with active communication, soliciting me to tickle her tummy, a social grooming pleasure often enjoyed between wolves and another kinship link between animal and man!

Wolf Touch

When a wolf is licked or groomed by a companion, or stroked by a person (which is the same thing if the wolf is bonded to that person), it will close its eyes in obvious ecstasy. Grooming and petting are solicited in a very distinct way by the wolf's approaching and turning sideways, often with the back slightly arched and the gaze directed downward and away from the companion; a few short whines may be given as well. Once contact is made, an extraordinary physiological reaction occurs. The heart rate slows down to half or less of its resting rate, a clear indication of arousal of the parasympathetic part of the autonomic or subconscious "vegetative" nervous system associated with pleasure. Contactual, tactile comfort is therefore a highly rewarding sensation and the wolves share this enjoyment with each other at all stages of their lives. Especially when a mother or babysitting "aunt" or "uncle" tends the cubs, when two wolves are enjoying courtship, or when two individuals in the pack share a particular allegiance, grooming occurs. Face, ears, neck, and shoulders are licked and gently nibbled, or nuzzled, and especially the skin fold in the groin area. One wolf will present its groin in a very clear display, as a friendly or appeasing gesture toward a companion, analogous somewhat to a human being offering his open palm to another to touch (or grasp and shake — a more recent culturally evolved derivation).

Taking turns grooming and being groomed is an intrinsic part of the social life of wolves, a reciprocal mode of expressing care and affection and giving pleasure to a companion. Similar behavioral and physiological changes occur in our "pets" — cats and dogs — when we pet them. Chimpanzees will spend six to eight hours a day giving each other tactile pleasure. Man, too, in courtship and in the tender loving touch of a mother and child, establishes and maintains a pleasure bond through this potent channel, through which care and love can be communicated and shared. The power of the laying on of healing hands has been long known and appreciated by man, and the devastating psychological and physiological effects of lack of tactile contact in developing infants have been more recently recognized.

The wolf shows us, as it does in and through its eyes, that touch is yet another channel of communication to experience and understand. With it we can directly reach across the illusory species barrier and know kinship and feel it flowing through our bodies as we touch.

Wolf Heart

That the heart rate drops so dramatically when a wolf is groomed or petted provides another clue whereby we can break through the apparent surface reality and discover subtle changes that occur from moment to moment within the very essence of the animal's being. Since such changes are not always apparent on the surface, so to speak, and although we may become attuned to them intuitively — as when someone's sudden change in breathing makes us feel breathless or anxious also — some creations of our space-age technology can help us explore the inner space of our fellow earth beings.

Using a small, specially tuned radio transmitter, a biotelemeter, with electrodes (the same kind as used on human beings) attached painlessly to a small area of shaved skin, changes in heart rate can be monitored via a radio receiver while the animal is free to

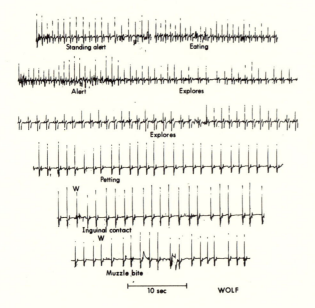

Standing alert   Eating

Alert   Explores

Explores

Petting

Inguinal contact

Muzzle bite

10 sec   WOLF

From a relatively fast heart rate when standing alert, the rate drops markedly when a wolf is exploring or paying attention to a novel stimulus. Even more dramatic slowing of the heart occurs when it is being groomed or petted, when the groin (inguinal) region is contacted, or when it is being subordinated and pinned to the ground by a social superior with a muzzle bite.

move and behave naturally. One can record the heart rate in a number of contexts without having to restrain the subject. The heart rate increases when the wolf is excited, by the sight of food for example, and when it is active physically. Subtle changes from a baseline resting level can be recognized, such as the slowing down of the heart rate when the wolf is stared at, which is a visual threat, when it "freezes" in fear or submission to a higher-ranking wolf, and, as mentioned earlier, when it is being groomed or petted.

Two other intriguing aspects of heart rate were brought to light in my research. One was the fact that the highest-ranking wolf — or cub — has the highest resting heart rate. It is as though the most alert, outgoing leader wolves have a different kind of autonomic nervous system tuning, a higher sympathetic tone. I have produced the same effect in domestic dog puppies through a regimen of mild stress early in life. Compared to littermates, the stressed pups had higher resting heart rates, were more outgoing, inquisitive, learned better (because they were less easily disturbed emotionally in unfamiliar situations), and became the dominant pups of their litters — just like the "alpha" wolf cubs.

Thus, although environmental stress or challenge (rather than over-swaddling) can produce marked changes in physiology and behavior, the early differences in wolf cubs, not given such stress, point to innate or genetic factors. The influence of such factors has a canalizing or determining effect, since one and two years later the most outgoing cubs with highest heart rates were still top of the pack. A former student of mine, Major Jeff Linn, with the Army Veterinary Corps, applied these findings to his work on breeding and training German shepherd "superdogs." He found that pups with higher resting heart rates tended, when older, to score better on tests used to evaluate trainability and stability of temperament.

Some people may feel that having a high heart rate could be a kind of "top dog" (or wolf) executive stress reaction. It would seem, however, that some wolves are basically better suited, both physiologically and psychologically, to be the alpha wolves — or executives — while others may be less preadapted and may be more susceptible to the stresses of assuming a particular social role.

The heart rate seems to be a reliable indicator that there are constitutional factors that influence, if they do not predetermine, how a particular wolf cub will mature socially and what role and rank it will assume in the pack. There is evidence that the heart rate may, however, change with a change in social rank (in chickens and squirrel monkeys), but perhaps the most intriguing thing to consider is the fact that the kind of autonomic nervous system "tuning" seems to have a potent and long-lasting influence on temperament, social rank, and relationships.

The other finding was that when a wolf is paying attention to some interesting stimulus, its heart rate declines dramatically. The identical phenomenon has been discovered in people also. But not all people are alike: two categories have been recognized, one reacting like the wolf, adapting slowly (low habituation) and constantly reacting with interest (and with a brief drop in heart rate) to anything interesting or novel in the environment. People reacting this way are called "sharpeners." The other class, termed the "levelers," show the same brief decline in heart rate when attending or "taking in" the environment, but this heart response wanes rapidly since these people habituate more quickly. Domesticated dogs tend to behave in a similar fashion, being less on the alert, as wolves are almost constantly, less responsive to unfamiliar, novel stimuli, and habituating very rapidly, both behaviorally and physiologically!

The heart rate also declines dramatically when a wolf is seized by the muzzle and is pinned to the ground by a superior. Such fear-bradycardia (heart-rate decline) is associated with passive "freezing" or tonic immobility in other animals (frogs, chickens, fawns) and may be an evolutionary antecedent of the bradycardia of active-submission greeting and friendly contact.

Which came first — the chicken-or-the-egg question — Does the cognitive and perceptual style of a person or wolf determine the kind of heart-rate response, or does the tuning of the autonomic nervous system influence the way we and wolves attend and respond? Evidence points to the latter prob-

*Scenes of motherhood: cubs cluster around the most productive groin teats;
mother takes the abuses of rough-playing cubs with calm understanding.
Attentive cubs wait as mother crushes a caribou marrow bone and mob her,
licking and pulling at her lips to solicit her to regurgitate meat.*

In more active displays of dominance, the alpha wolf will seize the jaws or muzzle of a subordinate and forcibly pin it to the ground. Active submission by the subordinate usually evokes such reactions.

ability, supporting the implication that the heart rate is also an indicator of early temperament and a predictor of later personality development on the basis of autonomic nervous system "tuning."

"Tuning" refers to the balance or equilibration between the two components of the autonomic nervous system, the sympathetic and parasympathetic, which increase and decrease the heart rate respectively. Already fairly well developed at birth, this system forms the basis for the subsequent development of emotional reactions, social relationships, temperament, etc. (for further details, see M. W. Fox, *Concepts in Ethology: Animal and Human Behavior* [Minneapolis: University of Minnesota Press, 1974]).

This fascinating and by no means fully explored research area leads us to the next topic already briefly exposed: the differences between wolf and dog, between being wild and domesticated. By comparing wolf and dog, the wolf can teach us what we have done to our closest animal companions and what, perhaps, in civilizing or "culturating" ourselves, we have actually done to ourselves also!

Wild, Tame;
Domestic and Civilized

While some people believe that the dog is a domesticated form of wolf, I believe that most breeds of dog are derived from a dingolike prototype and that wolf and dog are much more distant cousins. Even so, wolf and dog probably share a common ancestry in a now-extinct jackallike canid, and an intimate knowledge of the behavior and development of wolves and dogs can provide insights into domestication and wildness when the two are compared. We can discover then how nature has shaped the wolf (or rather, how the wolf has evolved and adapted to nature to become what it is) and how man has shaped the domestic dog to make it adapt to life with man. The process of domestication bears many similarities to culturation in man, where body structure, physiology, behavior, and psychology are modified in many subtle ways. Often these can

Wolves, like dogs, enjoy eating grass and chewing on and playing with sticks, the latter often being used as "social tools" catalyzing play between two or more pack members. Remains of prey, bones, antlers, and hide are also frequent play items for the pack and cubs.

only be recognized by studying a wild (wolf) prototype, or a "primitive" (at least technologically undeveloped) human culture, such as the African Bushmen or Australian aborigines.

We can only know with precision what we are doing to ourselves when we can step out of our enculturated or ethnocentric world view, since cultural "blind spots" prevent us from seeing and understanding how we influence ourselves and our future as well.

As an anthropologist totally immersed in an alien culture can reflect upon his own culture with a new clarity of vision, so for me, the wolf has provided many lessons on the nature of wildness. The wolf focused my knowledge of dog behavior and psychology in a new comparative dimension, providing a clearer picture of how domestication has changed the wolf's close cousin, the dog. The lessons from the wolf also gave me many insights about my own nature, not only because domestication of the dog and culturation of man are similar in many respects (and that man has made the dog in his own image!) but because in my prehistoric roots, part of my own essence as a hunter is socially and ecologically more akin to the wolf and its pack than to our closest primate relatives — gorillas and chimpanzees.* More about this will be said later. Domestication has caused the dog to increase its psychological dependence upon man so that it is easier to train: it becomes more of a conformist, anxious to please its human master or pack leader substitute. A wolf, however, even one that has been raised solely by man since before its eyes open, although it will regard its human foster parent as its pack leader, will never be as trainable as a domestic dog. This is the difference between being tame — not afraid of man and even socialized or emotionally bonded to him — and being domesticated. The dog is genetically or emotionally predisposed to bend to the human will, while the wolf, though affectionate and subordinate to its human pack leader, still retains a degree of independence and individuality that commands respect.

This basic difference between wolf and dog may be due to a form of psychosocial infantilism or neoteny — the perseverance of infantile dependence into maturity. Anthropologists also regard adult man as showing more infantilism or neoteny than his closest ape relatives, an intriguing parallel between domestication and culturation. Doglike dependence, trainability, and obedience, for many, though, may be self-limiting and lead to social repression and conformity, civilization and authoritarianism being common coincidences in the history of man.

* See R. L. Hall and H. S. Sharp, *Wolf and Man: Evolution in Parallel* (New York: Academic Press, 1978).

Wolf Sex

The sexuality of wolves, dogs, and men also shows some parallels. While the wolf may reach sexual maturity at two years of age, socially superior members of the pack will inhibit breeding at that age. Such nonbreeding adults serve the pack by tending the cubs — acting as babysitters and bringing food to them — i.e., undergoing a time of service and apprenticeship to their society before they have a family themselves. In human societies there is a similar social control of reproduction in fertile adolescents until they are fully adult, experienced and contributing members to society.

Domestication has greatly potentiated the dog's sexuality; a she-wolf is half as fertile as a female dog, the latter having two heats instead of one heat a year, as is the case in the wolf. A male dog is up to twelve times more fertile than a male wolf, the latter hav-

BARBARA VON HOFFMANN

After mating, alpha male and female remain tied and locked together, as with the domestic dogs, and the female howls softly. In this context, and also after a meal of favorite food, such howls may be interpreted as a sign of consummatory enjoyment.

Complexities of courtship: a male stands over its mate and solicitously grooms her and she may reciprocate. The male follows behind the chosen mate, who displays to him by leaning toward him with tail raised.

ing only a short four- to eight-week breeding season, whereas the domestic dog is constantly producing sperm. Dogs are also sexually precocious (maturing at six to nine months compared to a wolf's two- to three-year delay before sexual maturity) and are more promiscuous: wolves tend to have stronger mate preferences.

Man has wrought these changes in the dog through the process of selective breeding over many generations. One theory proposed by Russian scientist D. K. Baylaev (which he claims to have verified in his breeding studies of Arctic foxes) is that in selectively breeding only the most tractable animals, temperament changes resulted in hormonal changes. Docile animals have reduced adrenal gland activity and potentiated sex-hormone activity, while the reverse is true for those with "wild" or natural temperaments. Improved nutrition over several generations in captivity may also play a significant role in earlier sexual maturation and overall sexual potency.* The prime purpose of these changes in the dog (and also with cattle) was utilitarian; more offspring and more rapid selective breeding could take place with sexually precocious and superpotent stock. The subtle social, physiological, ecological, and seasonal factors that keep the wolf population in control are either lacking or are attenuated in the domesticated dog.

Domestication has similarly affected feline sexuality. The wild cat, like the wolf, has only one breeding season and males produce sperm only during the season; domestic toms are constantly potent and female cats have two or more heats per year (see M. W. Fox, *Understanding Your Cat*).

Some ethologists and anthropologists believe that sex, for man, is an essential part of a nonreproductive social and emotional bonding system. It is interesting and illuminating to see other species, such as the wolf and coyote, that stay together throughout the year independent of sex. Such an order of seasonal celibacy for all but two months of the year does not impair social bonds as it might in man, who has instead evolved a very

* For further details see M. W. Fox, *The Dog: Its Behavior and Domestication* (New York: Garland, 1978).

Subordinates of the pack intervene and mob the male (who is their father and the pack leader) in a display of obsequious friendly submission.

different sexuality. Wolves can enjoy mutual love and affiliation without year-round conflicts over and desire for sex. Perhaps if the reproductive consequences had been separated from the physical, emotional, and social needs and benefits of sex in our own evolution, it is unlikely that the biosphere today would be threatened by overpopulation of human beings. Wolves can stay together and love in their own way without sex, and do no harm to the earth. For our own well-being and for the good of earth we had best emulate the wolf, at least insofar as exercising a greater dominion over our sexuality and incredible reproductive potential.

In contrast to the domesticated dog and especially the "stud" dog, in which courtship behavior may be absent or perfunctory, wolf courtship is elaborate and extended over several weeks. After conflicts over sex-related social rank have been settled between the mature females of the pack and separately in the male ranks, a socially and emotionally compatible breeding pair emerges. This is often the top-ranking female and the number-one or -two male. The pair spend most of their time together, male attentively following and sniffing behind the female and driving off or staring down any other male who comes close. His mate will also subordinate any female who solicits him and she will aggressively intervene and prevent lower-ranking females from breeding with any other male in the pack.

While courtship is a time for considerable social vigilance, the couple enjoy frequent bouts of courtship play, reciprocal grooming, and lying close together. Males have been seen to bring gifts to their brides in the form of a freshly killed hare or a morsel of caribou or deer meat.

Wolves copulate and "tie" in the same way as dogs, and will mate more than once during the female's receptive phase. After the courtship and breeding periods are over, the pair retains its high pack status and maintains a strong bond that endures throughout pregnancy. When the cubs are born, the male will bring food to his mate and leave it by the den, and when the cubs emerge, he will assume fatherly duties of feeding, grooming, and playing with his offspring.

Communion of wolves. Two timber wolves howl together in a harmonizing chorus.

Wolves and Strangers

Wolves show a very distinct reaction toward strange wolves (and toward strange people, if the wolves are tame and have been raised in captivity), which is termed xenophobia. Such avoidance and fear of strangers is highly adaptive in the wild, since it keeps a pack together in a particular hunting range and thereby optimizes available resources in a given area. If the pack were "open" to strangers, or if its own members were to wander off and indiscriminately join up with neighboring packs, the consequences could be ecologically and economically disastrous. There might be too few wolves in the pack to hunt effectively or too many to feed for the carrying capacity of a given locale. Thus it is extremely valuable for the wolf pack to remain relatively closed and for xenophobia to be manifest in the presence of a stranger. Such is the case

A captive pack on the move together (leader with tail highest). Captive wolves, especially family groups, form the same kinds of complex, intrapack relationships and manifest the same behaviors (except cooperative hunting) as reported in the wild.

in primitive man also, since the balance of the tribe or clan population is critically tuned to available resources. Once culturation gained momentum, however, giving us more resources through developing agricultural practices and, more recently, through technological independence and affluence, it was no longer vital to keep the social group relatively closed to strangers. Greater interdependence between groups, and ultimately between regions and nations, for resources and the like, eroded the extended family and tribal structure. National identity took the place of tribal, familial and, to some extent, ethnic identity.

The human "pack," once so similar to the wolf pack's extended family composition, is something of the past. We may still yearn for it in our heterogeneous, unintegrated, anonymous urban societies where the nuclear family of husband, wife, and one or more children cannot fulfill our needs for deep and more varied kinship bonds.

Although society has changed, man has not, in his basic needs; the ancient

Wolf cubs at play: they quickly learn to avoid injuring companions with their extremely sharp milk teeth.

Two adult timber wolves: Always on the alert.

need for community — to be part of a pack or extended family — persists. Substitute "surrogates" for community (television, clubs, sports, hobbies, etc.) are only partially effective and the breakdown of the nuclear family — which without a supportive community is rarely optimal or "normal" anyway — is a symptom of modern man's increasing loneliness, alienation from anonymous groups, and lack of fulfillment through meaningful social relationships.

The wolf pack echoes our past way of life: togetherness, unity, kinship, cooperation, altruism, loyalty, obedience.

Another ancient reaction persists in man, which does not help him but which adds to his social and emotional dilemma of loneliness and alienation — namely, xenophobia. Getting to know someone involves an element of real or imagined risk, and an overfriendly person, if not appearing "pushy," at least puts one suspiciously on guard. Certainly the adaptive value of xenophobia, in keeping the tribe together, is an anachronism today and it is probably disappearing gradually, especially since our children are being more widely and diffusely socialized to others of different social, economic, and ethnic backgrounds.

Most breeds of dog have already made this transition. The lesson from the wolf here is that in the process of domestication, the xenophobia and limited capacities to develop secondary socialization (i.e., close ties with others later in life) of the wolf have been almost eliminated. In contrast to the wolf, the average dog is more than a "groupie" — it is open and accepting of virtually all strangers (unless it has been selectively bred and trained to be a more suspicious, as in the case of the xenophobic guard dog). Modern man, therefore, will probably become more and more like his dog in this regard, but his need for a few close friends — the kinship of the pack — may well persist, since without it, society may degenerate in decadent indifference, alienation, and competitive individualism. These symptoms are apparent today, and we must each find our own "pack," our own close community of like souls, sharing the same values, goals, and reciprocal affiliation and affection.

Wolf Brain

Apparently the human brain is about one-sixth smaller than it was in the late Pleistocene Age, when we lived by our wits, like wolves, as hunters. Some fear that our brains may become even smaller as we grow more dependent and even parasitic upon electronic "prosthetic brains" that "live" feel, entertain, move, think, and calculate for us. What might happen, ultimately, to human potentials because of these man-made creations is worth serious consideration. Is this aspect of culturation really limiting our potentialities and atrophying, rather than enhancing, our brains? These "prosthetic brains" do, at the least, take us away from the diverse and ever-changing natural environment to which our brains and potentials are preadapted and presumably best fulfilled. Charles Darwin drew similar inferences from his discovery that the domestic rabbit

The adaptation of the wolf physically, psychologically, and socially can best be appreciated when one sees the vastness of its terrain (Mount McKinley area, Alaska) and the size of some of its prey (a caribou bull).

has a smaller brain than its wild counterpart: the former, in a less varied, stimulating, and challenging environment, developed fewer of its potentials. Domestication and culturation may both lead to undesirable degeneration and inhibition of natural potentialities. Like modern and primitive man, the domestic dog has a brain one-sixth or so smaller than a wolf of comparable size. "Native intelligence" and temperament (where emotionality influences learning ability) also differ markedly between the wild and domestic canids. The latter, emotionally placid, relatively nonexploratory, take in less of their total environment (a "leveler," as noted earlier) than does the more finely tuned, reactive, and responsive wolf (a "sharpener"). The wolf's general alertness, its state of arousal, the exquisite sensitivity of its sense organs of hearing, smell, and sight, and its remarkable agility, dexterity, speed, and stamina demonstrate the phenomenon of natural adaptation. Through selection over generations to a hard and stressful environment, structurally, physiologically, psychologically, and socially, the wolf represents the fulfillment of all its adaptive potentials, a oneness with its environment being consummated in every aspect of its existence; nature knows best. Even the finest pure-bred dog can match the wolf in one or two attributes only, such as intelligence, speed, and stamina, or superb eyes or nose. Being domesticated or civilized relaxes and even protects dog and man from the rigors of natural selection, allowing for greater diversity in form and function and supporting variations from the structurally and psychologically adaptive norm, which could never survive under conditions in the wild. Some degree of protection or buffering from natural selection is evident, however, in the wolf pack, as in a human tribe, where certain individuals of a particular temperament could never hope to exist alone (and indeed some wolves may never actually kill prey themselves). For both wolf and man, belonging to the group can bring certain advantages for such

A wolf moves with grace and speed created by millennia of natural selection, a consummate expression of evolved perfection in the joy of movement.

individuals, whose presence adds to the diversity of the group, which greatly outweighs the pressures of conformity and having to belong in order to survive. A pathological degree of dependence may develop, however, in both domesticated dogs and culturated man, for supportive medication for example, and in the absence of positive selection pressures, degeneration both physically and psychologically may well occur. This is certainly true for many highly inbred strains of domesticated dog. Fortunately man does not inbreed, but the question remains for us: What are the best environmental conditions to optimize the development of a child's intelligence, sociability, physical ability, and overall mental and physical health? Through natural selection, wolf and man acquire those potentialities most conducive to adaptation, survival, self-actualization, and species continuation. What happens when the natural environment, to which we are genetically and to some extent culturally preadapted, suddenly changes? Is a highly artificial urban environment ideal for developing human potentials and what is needed to optimize human development? We have evolved from the natural world: Should we not still try to be a part of it? In nature we find not only our origins, but our fulfillment, as Paul Shepard in *Thinking Animals* so elegently describes. Rather than opt for a eugenics program of eliminating the social misfits, and the physically and psychically sick who cannot adapt, let us instead address the question of restoring our nature connectedness, within and through which is our significance and fulfillment. We can, and indeed should, support the poor, the weak, and the physically or psychologically "defective" members of our species. In such seemingly unnatural diversity may be much new potential. We should not dream of superraces: indeed the wolf is not a superrace. Although superbly adapted to its environment, the wolf's exemplary virtue for us to emulate is not cutthroat competitiveness but cooperation and social order. Like the wolves, we too can cooperate and work to realize our natural potentials in a world more conducive to human fulfillment that includes respect for nature and *all* life on earth, wolves and people of all races. Nature knows best and man should learn from nature and from these lessons from the wolf.

Wolf Space and Time

On the average, one wolf requires ten square miles of wilderness off which to live: thus, for a pack of fifteen wolves, the very minimum space requirement would be one hundred fifty square miles. In some habitats, where prey (caribou, moose) are scarce and widely dispersed, a wolf pack may have a hunting range of a thousand square miles or more. To cover such a vast area (and some varieties of wolf even travel thousands of miles following the migrating caribou) the wolf requires not only remarkable endurance, but must also have an intimate knowledge of its range: where prey are most likely to be found, most effectively stalked or ambushed, and so on. No other mammal has such an extensive range, nor perhaps the knowledge, presumably passed on "culturally" via observational learning by young cubs of their more experienced adult pack-

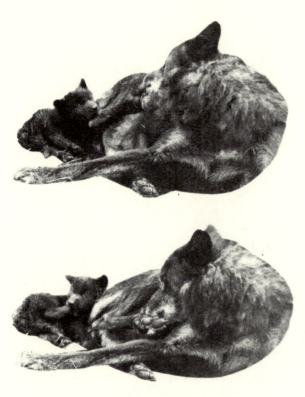

A coincidence or the key to culture? A wolf cub closely observes its mother grooming her paw and follows suit. Such a capacity for mimicry and observational learning may be essential for survival.

mates — except man. Even the most nomadic of the primates, the Savannah baboon, has a small foraging range of forty square miles, while man, as a nomadic hunter-gatherer, is much closer to the wolf in the range that is often covered. The Australian aborigine and American Indian acquired volumes of knowledge about the nature of the terrain and what and where food plants, water, and prey were most likely to be found.

In contemporary man, that almost ineffable wanderlust, the need for variety of places and of experiences, may well stem from an ancestral imperative to keep moving on within the familiar, but ever-changing, limits of relatively vast home ranges.

Another intriguing aspect of space is in the psychological and social dimension: personal space. Around each wolf is an invisible "balloon" such that every other wolf respects this inner personal space and will not violate it. For example, one wolf possessing a morsel of food will not usually be challenged by even a higher-ranking wolf: a zone some one to two feet around it is inviolable. Another more variable and extensive social space is also evident. High-ranking wolves have a greater social space than low-ranking ones and consequently have more social control and freedom. Identical phenomena have been identified in man also; and similarly, within

Displays of affectionate submission and allegiance to the leader: a wolf rolls over like a cub onto one side, and urinates; another bows (always approaching sideways, never head-on) and displays a submissive grin to the dominant snarl of the alpha wolf; an aloof alpha wolf ignores an actively submissive subordinate with an expressionless face of "passive indifference."

the innermost personal space, if actual physical contact is made, such contact is ritualistically confined to particular parts of the body in both man and wolf. Thus, one wolf may snuffle or lick the face, ears, or groin of another, or even gently seize its muzzle, while man will shake hands, pat shoulders, or embrace. Contact with other regions of the body — throat and shoulder in the wolf, and genitals in man — is taboo.

An even more striking analogy between wolf and man is the flight/fear space. In a wild, captive wolf that is not socialized to man, approach will elicit flight and, if the wolf is cornered, a defensive reaction may be triggered, which is termed the critical-distance reaction. Similarly, in psychotic states in man — in paranoid schizophrenia and in certain psychopathologies — the close proximity of a stranger evokes subjective feelings of fear and threat, and flight or aggressive reactions may be triggered.

A most remarkable consequence of the built-in time sense of animals (the circadian "clock") is the ability to navigate. Both homing and migration, especially in birds, is thought to involve a complex internal clock that facilitates the computation of direction afforded by environmental cues — solar, lunar, celestial, and geomagnetic. Such a sense of direction would be essential for the wolf with such a vast hunting range, and for "primitive" man, the hunter, as well. There are many documented cases of the uncanny directional sense of Eskimos, Plains Indians and Bushmen, often associated with a psychic awareness of where their nomadic companions may be. The wolf may well possess this latter psychic faculty, which has been reported in domesticated dogs and is referred to as psi-trailing.*

The faculty of homing-navigation in the wolf was clearly demonstrated recently in an experiment by some of my associates. Of a small pack of captive-born and -raised wolves released in a remote part of North Alaska, wearing radio-transmitting collars, one decided to return to its home cage. This wolf made an incredibly fast journey of almost two hundred fifty miles over completely unfamiliar terrain.

Scientists have recently discovered microscopic particles of an iron-containing material in the brains of pigeons. It is believed that this material could act as an internal geomagnetic compass and is the "missing link" that has been looked for to fill in the complex picture of the amazing homing and navigational abilities of birds. Perhaps the wolf and other mammals possess a similar magnetic direction sensor. Future research may elucidate this possibility, but an even greater challenge to the objectivity and technology of science is the question of psychic communication and psi-trailing

* See M. W. Fox, *Understanding Your Dog* (New York: Coward, McCann and Geoghegan, 1971).

in animals. I have no case histories of this latter phenomenon in wolves, but there are several examples from owners of cats and dogs. It is simply, and remarkably, this: the owners move to a new home, leaving the pet either at the old home with new owners or with friends nearby. Then, weeks and often hundreds of miles later, their pet arrives at their new home, never having been there before. Perhaps a lone wolf can "feel and see" where its companions are. Australian aborigines claim such psychic abilities when they go into an altered state of consciousness called "dream time." Is this an attribute of the natural mind, of the intelligence of man and wolf in the wilderness which we have all but lost in civilized ignorance of our true and natural potentials?

Wolf, Hunter and Hunted

Of the three other wolves in the release experiment just referred to, one was reported to have joined up with another pack of wolves, while the remaining two were shot by hunters. Possibly, because they were accustomed to people, they lacked the natural fear and avoidance of man and that led to their sad demise. Young wolves, more curious and less cautious than older ones, often fall to the hunter. But even the most wary and wise of wolves have little chance if caught out in the open in deep snow by a hunter in an airplane with high-powered rifle and telescopic sights.

The wolves in the experiment had been carefully released many miles from the nearest habitation but it is a sad reality that no wilderness area is far enough away from the hunter to make it a safe sanctuary for wildlife. A similar tragedy occurred in Michi-

The highest-ranking wolves usually eat first in the pack; altruistic food sharing is usually restricted to young cubs and social-rank-related priority over food has important ecological ramifications (see text for details).

gan where another colleague released a group of volves into an allegedly safe area, and even though in that state wolves are protected by the Endangered Species Act, they were shot by "sportsmen."

For many men, the wolf is the archetypal rival and the consummate trophy to bring home. For millennia, wolf and man have competed for the same ecological niche, both sharing a similar life-style as pack/tribal hunters. Respect and awe turned to hatred when man's life-style changed, when he ceased to be a kindred spirit living by his wits as a hunter and instead took the land himself. He took the land without forethought once he began his agrarian mode of life, his domesticated plants and animals having priority over all else. No longer did he share the land with his fellow creatures: wolves, eagles, pumas, elk, deer, bison, prairie dogs, American Indians, and countless other "rightful" residents, including the rich and varied flora, suddenly had no rights. As one great American Indian chief observed (a "primitive" though he was), the white man claimed the world for himself and did not see himself as an integral part of the world. It became an extension of his egocentric needs and values — an egosphere. This "superior"

*Developing the characteristic adult ruff around cheeks and neck, a yearling
she-wolf strikes a gentle, reflective mood.*

species, in its arrogant and blind indifference to wolf, Indian, and wilderness, is slow to learn that the ancient knowledge of so-called primitive people is the key to the ultimate wisdom of nature. Our ignorance of nature not only endangers ourselves and all sentient beings alike, it also denies us fulfillment in and through nature on which we are physically and psychologically extremely dependent. Even the humanocentric and ethnocentric notion of man's superiority — or suggesting that the wolf is superior to and more highly evolved than the deer that it hunts — serves to separate and alienate man from nature, or one species "above" or "below" another. Thus the seeds of our own destruction are sown in such concepts, values, and attitudes; and we reap racism, prejudice, exploitation, "speciesism," sexism. While man may be more *continuously* evolving than the wolf, that only makes us different and not superior, and more responsible to other life forms with less freedom of will to determine their future existence than we have.

Why then does man continue to persecute the wolf and take pleasure in killing it for "sport"? Some antagonists suggest that the hunter derives sexual gratification or catharsis of pent-up aggressive urges. But most likely, the reason has recently been revealed by the hunters themselves. In a survey of duck hunters conducted by the United States Fish and Wildlife Service, the conclusions were generalized to include all hunters and summarized as follows:

. . . while hunting provides many different satisfactions, most of them are also present in other activities. Especially relevant for hunting, however, is the thrill of engaging in a contest with wild creatures — in no other way can man participate so directly in nature as by putting his cunning, skill, or stamina against game animals. Killing the animals is an integral part of the satisfaction, not because of bloodlust but because until the animal is killed the hunter cannot fully feel that he succeeded in winning the contest. If he stops short of killing and lets the game go free, then the game did not, after all, lose the contest. In a genuine contest, if there is to be a winner there must be a loser, and the only way an animal can "acknowledge" that it lost is to be shot.*

This statement adequately depicts the immaturity of ego manifest by the hunter: to "participate so directly with nature" — some *contest* indeed against ducks or deer — "putting his cunning, skill or stamina against game animals."

Interestingly, the survey adds that the cost of bringing meat home, in terms of equipment, time, licenses, etc., far outweighs the value of the meat, thus stressing (unintentionally, no doubt) that such hunting is no more than a luxury sport and a most uneconomical way of feeding one's family!

* "Why Hunters Hunt," *Outdoor Life* (May 1976).

The dominant mates of a captive pack consuming a deer carcass. Lower ranking pack members (waiting in background) eat later.

Wolf following deer tracks in winter.

Clearly the trophy hunter and the "sportsman" who kills predators such as the wolf must be helped and encouraged, as one would a child, to mature beyond his limited egocentric world view. To see what is between the sights of his gun and to claim it for himself is a grossly selfish misperception, especially since the killing of wolves is not essential for man's survival but serves only for his immediate gratification.

The hunter has learned one lesson from the wolf: namely, that without the predator, deer and other game would become too numerous and would suffer a population explosion and crash. Many hunters see themselves, therefore, as wolves, as "managers" playing a vital role in maintaining the balance of nature. Using this as their main rationale for hunting — that they help conservation — still does not satisfy the primary ethical questions of man's killing for pleasure and of eliminating natural predators so man can enjoy all for himself. No wolf kills for pleasure; it must kill in order to live, a justification few human hunters can offer. After all, we have taken so much from nature in developing the land for our own domesticated plants and animals that today non-subsistence and trophy hunting is surely an anachronism for Western man.

Wolves and Men, Women, and Children

It is almost as though a wolf can sense instinctively that man — or men, more correctly — is a hunter. Many people who have kept wolves in captivity have commented on their general fear and wariness toward males of our species, even when they have been hand-raised by a man and are well socialized. With women, wolves are less fearful and are often so friendly that they will attempt to solicit play and keep a female human visitor in the cage. Children evoke obvious excitement and curiosity in the wolf. Some wolves, without social control, might accidentally injure a child by engaging in excessive mouthing and rough play. Other wolves seem more aware of their own size and strength and are extremely gentle and passive with children, even permissive, allowing a child, as they would a wolf cub, to pull on tail and ears and generally

A wolf scans the woods for its companion, and howls in order to locate him.

have more social freedom within their personal space than any adult wolf or human might — unless the former were mate or pack leader.

Since the wolf's social evolution has favored the selection of strong parental tendencies, such reactions toward children — and toward coyote cubs, kittens, and puppies — are not surprising. Yearling wolves — both males and females — will act parentally and assist an older wolf in raising its offspring, assuming the roles of indulgent and protective aunts and uncles. One of my own yearling wolves tore down a strong partition in order to get into an adjacent enclosure simply so that she could be with six two-month-old coyote cubs. Long before sexual maturity (and therefore without any prior experience of parenting) young wolves will spontaneously regurgitate meat to feed infant animals — be they wolf cubs or the offspring of other carnivores such as jackal, coyote, and domestic dog. With such a strong, natural parental instinct and a clear awareness of what is infantile, it is not difficult to find support for the legend of Romulus and Remus and other wolf-child stories. What detracts from such possibilities is the immaturity of the nursling child and its limited capacities to adapt to a wolf foster parent, rather than the reverse.

Wolves and Men, Women, and Children

Fuzzy fur makes just-emerged, 24-day-old cubs almost invisible as they follow their mother. Yearling packmates greet and investigate them with gentle curiosity. When older, these cubs solicit a yearling to regurgitate food and when subadult, the top-ranking cub follows father (the pack leader) and maintains a close allegiance.

Roles of motherhood: meticulous grooming of cubs, regurgitating food for them, and carrying food to them.

Trust and affection between a wolf and a boy who have grown up together.
Note similarity of facial expressions.

Having accounted teleologically for the wolf's natural acceptance of human infants, their different reactions toward adult men and women are more difficult to interpret.

After carefully observing how men and women usually behave when they approach a tame wolf, I offer the following interpretation, which is based upon the thesis that men and women differ in the way they perceptually and cognitively engage with and respond to certain features of their environment. This difference has been wrought by hundreds of thousands of years of selection, of sex-correlated, if not sexually determined, division of labor into respective roles of male-hunter, female-gatherer (and food-preparer and baby-carer). The male scans and "penetrates" the environment perceptually and cognitively, while the female is more passive-receptive, i.e., "taking in" the environment. These ancient roles and related perceptual and cognitive styles of male and female are reflected in contemporary men and women in their different psychophysical modes. These modes affect overt behavior and reactions such that a wolf will respond differently to men and women. Expressing forcibly in body language "I want to be friendly with you," and imposing one's intentions upon the animal, usually evokes

Wolves, socialized to man, respond to children in much the same gentle and understanding way as they would to their own cubs.

Wolves and Men, Women, and Children /

On first meeting, a wolf accepts a totally strange human female (note reciprocal postures and facial expressions) but would respond initially with fear toward a strange human male, and warm up very slowly and cautiously.

flight or, occasionally, defensive aggression or passive submission. Squatting, remaining quiet, not staring directly (which is threatening to a wolf), and expressing with one's body language and whole presence "Come to me and let us be friends" usually break the initial fear/flight reaction and friendly contact is established. This latter approach I regard as a typically empathetic passive-receptive "female" mode.*

One must also consider the role of odor in affecting a wolf's reaction toward men and women. I feel that a wolf probably becomes differentially conditioned to these odors secondarily to the initial experience of being intimidated by an imposing male "hunter."

The perceptual and cognitive style of children, who are essentially "diffusely" open, receptive, and with a constantly shifting focus or attention, creates less tension in a wolf; children tend "to take it in" rather than "go into it." A direct stare, a raised arm and hand pointing at a wolf, or even a camera pointed at it can be extremely disturbing and trigger passive submission, avoidance of eye contact, or fear and flight. Such human actions, consciously or unconsciously, may be a focusing of one's behavior into a directed energy or force that impinges upon the animal. In the body language of the wolf, such behavior is a threatening, assertive, or dominant display.

I often wonder if wolves react differently to different people because they can detect, especially through the person's body language, how they are being perceived subjectively. The wolf, a highly sensitive, experienced, and intuitive ethologist in its own right, may be able to sense quite accurately how a person is feeling toward it, just as it can with a fellow pack male.

For the past several years, I have regularly taken a wolf out for exercise on a leash to the local park and the reactions of people are particularly enlightening. Generally the younger the person, the less prejudice, negative mythos, and catastrophic expectations are voiced. Children are usually more cognizant and sensitive and sensible than adults; among adults, women are more so than men. The wariness and fear that most wolves show toward adults, especially men, and their friendliness toward children, may be related to this. Wolves may detect fear and prejudice in a person's body language and tone of voice.

One would expect that the more mature a person becomes, the more he or she would know, or at least the more aware he or she should be, and the more in control of fears and catastrophic expectations. It would seem that it takes several years for the "big bad wolf" myth to sink in. But once such prejudices and fears are established, a void is created conceptually between

_____

* Which any male can assume: these male–female differences are more archetypal than sex stereotypes.

man and animal, and in relation to man and wolf, the wolf is aware of this void and will avoid contact or even close proximity with such a person.

I would like to believe that a generation or so ago, children were as fearful and wary of wolves as many adults are today, and that the unprejudiced curiosity, awe, and affection that children do show toward wolves today is a consequence of good education — of the objective scientific knowledge about the nature of wolves and other wild animals at last reaching the classroom and eliminating the negative myths that parents and children's fairy tales transmit from generation to generation. Perhaps, at last, we are seeing a reduction in this form of civilized ignorance, thanks to the dissemination of factual information.

The lesson from the wolf — that men, women, and children must be behaving differently in order to evoke such very different reactions — warrants further study from the point of view of understanding human behavior and the dynamics of wolf–human interaction.

As mentioned earlier, wolves of superior social rank have a greater social distance control and social space (or freedom) than those of lower status, while cubs are given a high degree of social freedom. The body language and demeanor, which includes individual physiology and temperament and also social and personal space variations, differ for each individual wolf in the pack. Also, one pack may have a very different ambience from another. I will discuss these important individual and pack differences next.

Wolves as Individuals, and Pack Dynamics

Individual differences in basic temperament and physiology (as in the heart rates described on pages 13–18) can be recognized in very young cubs. Such differences within the litter are important because if every cub were to be a submissive follower or a strong-willed leader, pack formation would be virtually impossible. The heterogeneity of developing personalities in a litter forms the basis of a future pack, each cub maturing into a particular rank and role within the complex and dynamic social context of the pack. While Kipling aptly wrote that the strength of the wolf is in the pack and the strength of the pack is in the wolf, we must add that the strength of the pack lies also in the diversity of its individual members. We know too that for optimal performance, productivity, or creativity, a human group is best made up of people with differ-

No wolf should be alone in captivity: it is a highly social species and needs the companionship of its own kind.

At three weeks of age, a wolf cub is more like its bear cousin than the long-nosed and lithe creature it is to become.

A curious young wolf cub approximately nine weeks of age emerging from the den.

ent skills, attributes, and viewpoints, united in spirit by a common goal.

Kipling, even though he was not an ecologist or animal behaviorist, knew intuitively that the wolf pack is a gestalt — where the whole is greater than the sum of its parts. Collectively, the pack can transcend the physical limitations of the individual and cooperatively secure large prey that no wolf could bring down alone. The range and variation of temperaments provide a diversity of abilities which collectively make for a supraintelligence. Similarly, man, as an individual, is limited.

One cub, often the largest and usually the most inquisitive and confident of the litter, can be easily identified as the initiator, instigator, and charismatic catalyst of social interactions within the litter and with novel objects, including play toys (bones, antlers, etc.) and small prey (insects, rodents, etc.). Less outgoing and more timid cubs show an increasing tendency to follow such a cub. As the cub matures, its followers' dependency creates its role of pack leader. In other words, the basic temperament of the wolf cub (in this example the future pack leader) is canalized or shaped by the social environment within the pack and a social role and individual personality eventually emerge.

The pack leader is often referred to as the dominant or alpha wolf. The former term, implying some form of aggression, is misleading, since many leader wolves are less aggressive and probably more secure than some lower-ranking wolves. Also the less assertive the leader is, the less likelihood there is of dominance fights and aggression in the pack. The general demeanor or ambience of the pack is very much determined by the personality of the lead wolf (who is perhaps best regarded generally as a benevolent despot). One pack may have a relaxed and easygoing ambience because the lead wolf is a friendly and playful individual and on good terms with all the wolves. In another pack there may be an "upper echelon" of the leader and one or two others who have a close allegiance, and another wolf in the pack who is often in conflict with the leader. The upper echelon may help repress such an upstart but the pack as a whole may manifest more social tension as a consequence. In some packs the leader may be constantly having to be assertive, and aggressive interactions are common. Such a pack ambience may be due to the onset of the breeding season when one or more lower-ranking wolves are vying for the alpha position.

Nor is there a simple linear rank or dominance hierarchy ("pecking order") per se. Within the pack there are usually certain alliances among individual members that are not restricted by age or sex. In two captive packs, for example, the cub with the most leader-role potential was a constant companion of the pack leader, following it everywhere, while its littermates kept more to themselves. Close allegiance with a high-ranking individual may be an assurance of high social status (a fact well known by

Anxiously defensive, a low-ranking wolf cub takes its share. Dominance fights are rare in young cubs; note the assertive display of a dominant cub standing over a subordinate, both aged five weeks, the latter showing a clear submissive grin. Biting during play (lower pair) is under remarkable social control.

Wolves as Individuals, and Pack Dynamics / 59

Wolf cubs grown from short-muzzled, stubby-eared, bearlike creatures (at twenty-four days) to gangling juveniles with heads and feet out of proportion (four months) to almost full-scale adult proportions (twelve months).

Social Organization
of the
Wolf Pack

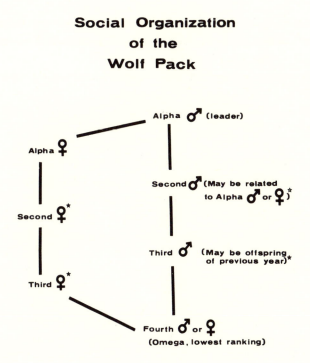

human "social climbers!"), but it may also reflect an intriguing element of reciprocal compatibility of personalities or of complementary and supporting qualities of temperament. This humanistic area of compatibility and social preferences warrants further study in wolves, especially in terms of mate preferences. Studies of preferences for play partners suggest that wolf cubs of similar temperament and arousability prefer to play together, while a pair where one partner is less assertive or slower to warm up may not be so compatible. Often during play, however, social roles may be reversed, thus complicating the picture of a simplistic model of reciprocal compatibility; a high-ranking wolf may temporarily assume a subordinate role and allow a low-ranking wolf to chase it and playfully attack and dominate it. Then, too, there is the unexplored area of deception and social manipulation, as when one wolf solicits play in order to distract its companion and steal its food!

Living closely with wolves gives one continuous insights about their perceptions and changing relationships. The following observations of one of my wolves raise many questions. Although hand-raised, she was a relatively normal wolf, having lived with a captive pack for over a year. She was also socialized to dogs, living with one and meeting new and familiar dogs on daily walks in a nearby park. Between seven and eight years of age, she added a new dimension to her clear dislike for female dogs and powerful instinct to subordinate (but not kill) them. She began to react in the same way toward very old male dogs and also toward castrated males. With very small (ten-to fifteen-pound) to medium-sized (twenty- to thirty-pound) male dogs, she was often ambivalent, occasionally being friendly and at other times either indifferent or ready to pin them to the ground and force submission. With normal adult male dogs (thirty pounds and up) she was invariably friendly and often extremely solicitous and submissive. How much this aggressive behavior toward small, old, and neutered male dogs is an artifact and how much a reflection of natural wolf-to-wolf behavior is debatable. Could this kind of behavior be an adaptive response to eliminate senile, sterile, or otherwise abnormal wolves from the pack? Further field studies may answer this question. There are obvious economic and genetic advantages in eliminating noncontributing and physically abnormal wolves from the pack.*

Relationships also change as wolves die, attain sexual maturity, or strike up new allegiances. Against a constantly changing background of individuals and relationships over generations, the unity of the pack is maintained throughout by the enduring bonds of social attachment, of allegiance, and the inborn tendency to follow the leader. Xenophobia, discussed earlier, also serves a societal function, helping to maintain pack allegiance. Packs do sometimes break up; occasionally this is seasonal, as when the type and abundance of prey necessitates smaller hunting units. Individuals will sometimes leave the pack, and these are not inferior or aged "outcasts." Some may be young adult wolves with "leader" temperaments, who, because of social repressions or conflicts within the pack (especially around the spring breeding season), choose not to stay. The fate of such loners is not fully known; they may provide an essential gene flow between neighboring packs, which would help regulate excessive inbreeding, providing they were able to gain acceptance into a strange or relatively unfamiliar pack. Some loners may find a loner mate (or lure one) from another pack and, if conditions are optimal, establish their own pack.

Little is known yet about the genetic and social relationships among packs: it is probable that all packs in a given area are genetically related (i.e., forming a regional subspecies), but the extent to which wolves of different packs know each other remains to be determined. An old grandfather, for example, who knew a wolf when it was a cub before the pack split in two, or a loner brother in a neighboring pack could maintain some form of kinship ties between packs. My research with captive wolf packs in Alaska, where wolves from separate packs and of different ages were introduced into

* Recently this same wolf solicited a large male dog, then suddenly attacked. I learned from its owner that it had just been playing with two female dogs.

*As the alpha wolf (center) pins a subordinate in a ritualized display of rank,
another wolf (second from right) displays its submission to a higher-ranking
companion. Such "chain effects" or redirections are common in social animals.*

*The pack greeting ritual: subordinates surround the leader and display
active submission while he stands with tail crest and head high in the center.
Such a group "love-in" often precedes a hunt and may be followed by a pack
chorus of howling.*

different packs, supports this possibility. One old male who knew, as cubs,
two other wolves from different litters actually served as a peacemaker when
the two wolves, who had never been with each other before, were introduced. In the presence of the "old man" they were friendly to one another
and subordinate to him. In his absence, they fought each other.

There is a remarkable parallel between pack size and the size of a tribe
or band of primitive human hunter-gatherers, both maintaining, by necessity, a group size comparable with or lower than the carrying capacity (i.e.,
food supply) of the habitat. Population regulation in the wolf seems to be
effected by a form of social birth control. Usually only the dominant female
breeds, and she will prevent others from mating. The lead male is not
always her mate; she may, for example, choose a second-ranking male who,
if on good terms with the leader, may consummate the relationship. If food
is scarce, competition may erupt and low-ranking, often young wolves, may
starve or be forced to leave the pack nucleus in search of food. In man,
selective infanticide and gerontocide are ancient and adaptive strategies,
as are taboos on intercourse while a child is being nursed, which may be
for an effectively long period. A social form of birth control analogous to
that of the wolf also operates in man, where subordinate fertile adolescents
are not allowed to marry and procreate until they attain a certain age and
are contributing economically to the community.

Wolves do not exist in tropical regions where food is abundant year round.
The wolf, and probably the periglacial Stone Age man, adapted socially to a
much less hospitable environment, territoriality being essential for survival.

Yearling wolves (above) engage in an early morning greeting ritual and (below) are soon joined by a litter of cubs and their mother in a pack display of togetherness.

If packs or bands did not respect each other's territory, and if social groups were not maintained at a fairly constant size in a given hunting range, survival would be threatened. In times of acute shortage of food, a stronger wolf pack will drive another pack out and occupy that pack's hunting territory, as well as its own.

That the strength of the wolf is in the pack, and vice versa, implies that there must have been a strong social selection for certain attributes, just as there would have been in man as a hunter. Man and wolf share such attributes as loyalty and obedience (to the leader), strong social bonds of kinship and group allegiance, empathy and altrusim, including care of an injured adult (which has been observed in the wolf) and care of another's offspring (which belong as much to the pack as to the parents). Empathy and compassion would also be important qualities having a high selection priority since, for both wolf and man, they would favor survival.

Control of aggressive impulses — through ritual displays and submission — are seen in both man and wolf. The hierarchical social organization itself reduces conflict, since each individual knows his or her own particular place in relation to the focal leader or "control" wolf. The latter will even intervene and settle disputes between lower-ranking packmates, an important policing or control role.

A wolf ritual also common to many human cultures is a group display of allegiance where the leader is affectionately greeted and submitted to. I'll discuss body language associated with such rituals and the more subtle modes of communication later; there are some social and political aspects of wolf and human society it would be appropriate to consider first.

Wolf Pack and Politics

The wolf pack is neither a model for communism nor a monarchy nor a democracy, although a limited monarchy perhaps most closely describes its structure in human terms. With a leader or control wolf, a dominance (or submission) hierarchy, an upper echelon of high-ranking wolves, a more loosely structured middle-rank, and a tendency for individuals to assume certain social roles (which change with age and also as the pack composition and structure change), the wolf pack is a complex phenomenon. It is difficult, therefore, to make analogies with existing sociopolitical systems evolved by man, although the similarities between the wolf pack and the clans and bands of early man, still evident in many contemporary cultures, are founded on a common basis: the extended family. Leadership, kinship, allegiance, obedience, conformity, altruism, and cooperative individualism are manifest attributes and imperatives in the pack and clan systems alike. A monarchy with the seeds of responsible communism and democratic freedom: loyalty and social order, involving responsibility toward others and the pressures of socializing conformity. Limited and conditional personal freedom is balanced by the enhanced survival through unity, and herein are the seeds of egalitarian self-fulfillment.

Any social system of man or animal is subtly altered and adapted to environmental-economic restraints and potentialities. For the wolf pack, one must think in terms of survival, of individual fulfillment, and of continuation of the species, and appreciate the subtle balance between the individual and the pack.

Sociopolitically and ideologically man has polarized from this natural wolf model into two extremes. Capitalism and competitive individualism, with the growth of multinational corporations and control of many by a powerful few, have grown from the seeds of democracy in the West. The balance between personal freedom and commitment to and concern for the welfare of society as a whole is breaking down. The other extreme, communism, initially no less democratic in its promise of personal freedom and fulfillment through society, has, in most countries, become a denial of personal freedom and repression of social mobility and flexibility. The bureaucracies running the socioeconomic system are more concerned about the system itself than about the actualization of each individual.

Thus, capitalistic individualism on the one hand (like a disintegrated pack of alpha wolves) and communism on the other (like a herd of sheep or repressed pack of omega wolves) have failed. Socially and psychologically we may be closer to the wolf than we realize and our survival and fulfillment may come when we can integrate the positive aspects of individualism and communism, a true democracy based upon personal freedom and responsibility.

At a more personal family level, we may also be happier and healthier psychologically if we can reestablish a sense of local community. This would be an effective substitute for the extended family and would provide for more enrichment and fulfillment than can the nuclear family alone and alienated in the no-man's-land of suburbia, in comfortably isolated indifference to the outside world. Without the establishment of such community "packs," concern for local and regional economic, environmental, and political issues could never be coordinated into community-action programs. We would be alienated and impotent indeed, since the political strength of man is in the community and the strength of the community is in the commitment and responsibility of each one of us. Only through a sense of community, growing from within these separate centers of awareness and involvement, can a true democracy flourish. And without community, the future would be indeed bleak for the conservation, humane and human rights movements, and the like, since the machinery to effect social change would be nonexistent. Democracy is an egalitarian system run for the benefit of all people, by all people. As each wolf has its place in the pack, so too must each of us find our place in the sociopolitical structure that affects our lives and future. To be noninvolved is to be an egocentric loner. If wolves were this way, they would not exist today. And we may not exist tomorrow, since the most destructive force to a democracy is not communism or corporate control but competitive individualism (I'm OK, to hell with you) and indifference, apathy, and alienation.

Wolf "Social Tension"

Wolves' reactions to dogs and to their own kind occasionally give us fleeting insights into the wolf's nature. Cubs that grow up with an adult domestic dog will often remain subordinate to it, even when they have grown much larger and stronger. Adult wolves will frequently challenge strange adult dogs of the same sex and be friendly toward those of the opposite sex. One female wolf, who had been neutered and therefore had no further heat cycles, would usually court large male dogs but ignore or threaten smaller adult males. Two young male wolves socialized to both dogs and wolves showed (at one and two years of age) a rather bizzare response when introduced to a strange adult female wolf and a strange adult male dog. They ignored or threatened the wolf and showed active submission and play behavior with the dog. The strange female wolf would have responded to male dogs of comparable size with play and quasi-courtship actions but she ignored these two wolves. She had at an earlier age lived with other wolves in a pack.

The impression gained from the overt wolf-to-wolf aversion and the social preference for the adult male dog was that the dog was seen as being nonthreatening. In spite of the sociability of wolves, as adults they are tense around other strange wolves and subjectively have to keep up appearances or put on a face, so to speak, with other wolves. But with a dog, they can be themselves; there is less social tension. This may be related to the fact that dogs, even as adults, are generally more infantile in certain behaviors and ritualized displays. Is such domestication-induced infantilism in the dog sensed by the wolf as nonthreatening? While a strange dog may act as a social catalyst and cause social attraction, a strange wolf may cause social tension and avoidance. When strange wolves are placed together in the same enclosure, dominance fights occur (since there is no escape), but a tightly knit pack structure rarely develops.

In order for a pack to form, the wolves, even from different unrelated litters, must have been raised together from early in life. As adults, wolves have a natural tendency to be attracted to their own packmates and to avoid or threaten strange wolves, reactions that may help maintain inter- and intrapack stability in the wild.

This may be the reason why the three wolves mentioned above avoided each other, but does not explain why those two young male wolves should enjoy playing with a strange adult male dog. The most logical conclusion is that the domestic dog was socially attractive and was perceived as nonthreatening, a conclusion confirmed on numerous occasions by John Harris, who has observed similar reactions in wolves toward strange wolves and dogs.

Between-Pack Politics

A particularly intriguing aspect of wolf-pack "politics" or territoriality has been recently discovered by L. David Mech in his studies of Minnesota wolves. The neutral, no-man's zone between adjacent wolf packs serves as a refuge for deer. Contiguous wolf packs avoid hunting in the neutral zone in order to avert confrontation with the neighboring pack, which could result in injury and death. The wolves benefit indirectly from this because a breeding pool to repopulate their hunting range with deer is always available. Always, that is, with the rare exception of when one wolf pack takes over the territory of another, driving the residents away and incorporating the deer "refuge" into their expanded territory. Under such circumstances a number of deer may come to inhabit the neutral zone at the edge of the wolves' expanded territory. They would once again be a protected population, buffered by the territoriality of neighboring wolf packs. This naturally evolved preservation of wildlife would be an excellent model for us to emulate in conserving wildlife in buffer zones between centers of human activity. Mech and co-worker Fred H. Harrington also find that wolf howling plays an important role in interpack politics, serving to maintain and advertise territorial occupancy. They concluded that wolves are more likely to howl to proclaim territoriality when they have made a kill, have a litter of pups, or are alpha individuals. Also they stated:

Howling was considered most effective in mediating avoidance in two situations: when two packs approached a common area of overlap, and when a pack returned to an area little used for weeks, in which scent posts would have lost effectiveness in deterring strangers. Both scent-marking and howling apparently are important in spacing. However, they differ in their roles and are complementary, with scent-marking being long-term and site-specific, and howling being immediate and long-range.

Wolf Body Language

The first and most obvious impression that one gets about the character and social status of people is in the way in which they walk, carry themselves, make or evade eye contact, and so on. Body demeanor gives an instantaneous (often like-dislike) impression about personality, and such first impressions are often confirmed when one gets to know a person a little better. Such subtle unconscious body language, as I have detailed elsewhere,* is a composite of habitual posture and gesture, "frozen" displays (of fear, association, etc.), and attitudes (of defeat, self-confidence, etc.). The same is true in the wolf: at once one can usually pick out the leader wolf by its impressive carriage; with head and tail high, the leader *looks* and be-

* See M. W. Fox, *Between Animal and Man: The Key to the Kingdom* (New York: Coward, McCann & Geoghegan, 1976).

A captive wolf pack: the omega or lowest-ranking member can be easily identified by its more permanent tail-and-ear-down display or role-related attitude (far right).

Contrast in facial expressions reflecting changes in emotional states: smiling wolf hugs a malamute dog in courtship and displays an open-mouthed play face when he (more hesitantly) reciprocates. Offensive threat (snarl and

haves its role to the full. Also the lowest-ranking, or omega, wolf can be easily identified by its skulking, cowering posture and gait; with tail, ears, and head lowered, it usually avoids eye contact with others and acts submissively toward almost all of the other wolves. Segregating those of intermediary rank can be difficult because of the complexities of allegiance between ages and within and between the sexes. One way is to record the number of times each wolf threatens or challenges another (over food) and wins. Sometimes, though, a clearly high-ranking wolf just isn't interested and lets the other have its way, or more subtly ignores its threat with a blank, inscrutable expression of passive indifference. A more reliable way to find out who is who in the hierarchy is to record the number of submissive displays each wolf gives and receives. A submissive display can range from rolling over onto one side, to urinating like a puppy, with ears back and a clear submissive grin (with lips retracted horizontally like a "hi, boss" smile of an office peon to the chief executive), to a more active greeting. This includes whining, licking and/or pawing at the other wolf's face, and tail wagging. Instead of remaining supercool and aloof, the submitted-to wolf may growl and seize its fawning companion by the muzzle and pin it to the ground. This may seem like a violent and aggressive response but it is a highly controlled display of superiority, which has evolved from an aggressive action into a more affectionate or socially cohesive affiliative behavior. The dominant wolf will often

small, puckered mouth) contrasts with the more open gape of defensive-aggressive display in a lower-ranking wolf.

whine (solicitously or indulgently) while pinning the other with its jaws and may subsequently behave like a parent and actually lick up the urine voided by the subordinate (who has "regressed" to behave like a piddling puppy). The subordinate wolf may sometimes approach a superior and solicit such a reaction; being seized by its muzzle and pinned to the ground is not sadomasochism but a subtly evolved reciprocal ritual of allegiance to the leader ("You are my superior parent/leader"; "Yes, I am your superior parent/leader"). A tape recording of the growls, whines, and whimpers made during such an interchange sounds like a bloody, bullying feud; but it is beyond bluff — it is the essence of ritual.

To refocus these lessons from the wolf, we see in man similar ritualistic interchanges between highly esteemed social superiors and followers, or subordinates. The former have social freedom in initiating greetings and other activities and take the prerogative in making decisions and the like. They can be picked out of a group not only by the deference (or submission) others display toward them, but also, as with the wolf, by the focus of attention and eye contact that is directed to the leader. Body language "in the ranks" is worth observing: the assertive social climbers (often seeking close proximity to the leader and mimicking his behavior and decisions); the followers nodding in agreement; the skeptics ready to assert their individuality and perhaps form their own pack or dissident faction; the subordinate yes-men, who check to see who is nodding or otherwise displaying

Sadomasochism? No: a ritualized display of active submission (derived possibly from face licking to solicit food), which is reciprocated by the alpha wolf's gently seizing the subordinate's muzzle in a snarling display of controlled power and high rank.

The "wolf kiss": unmoved and displaying an expression of indifference, the alpha wolf looks into the far distance as a subordinate gives it a friendly nuzzle.

A wolf enjoys rolling on a deer carcass before eating. Such behavior may be a sign of olfactory aesthetics: wolves, like dogs, seem to enjoy "wearing" certain odors, especially of carrion.

A wolf well insulated by its winter coat sleeps through a blizzard.

agreement or allegiance with the leader or upper echelon — the sheep of the pack. Enough analogies; suffice it to say that, discounting what is said in favor of how it is said, and also discounting the frequency and form of body language, one can see the same social dynamics and analogous behaviors in human groups as are seen in the wolf pack.

An even more dramatic analogy is the fact that an individual wolf's or person's body language and whole demeanor changes with a change in social rank/self-esteem. A low-ranking wolf who becomes leader will manifest a complete change in behavior and personality with its new role. So will man, up to a point, since the stigmas of habit and more frozen attitudes of character structure are the somatic burdens of our species — sometimes crippling indeed. The wolf demonstrates the phenomena of both social and psychological flexibility, and although we, in a democratic society, may enjoy the former, we tend to be somewhat deficient in the latter. A person attaining the highest point in his profession will carry in his body language the somatic scars and residues of past social roles, anxieties, and traumas.

Anyone seeing a wolf move, in its long, open, effortless lope or racing at full speed, or twist and turn on one foot, will admire, if not envy, its agility and coordination. Mind and body are one, totally integrated, and few dogs can match the liquid movements, speed, and stamina of the wolf. Those dogs bred by man to match the wolf in speed lack the flexibility and equipoise of the wolf. Relaxed, a wolf *looks* relaxed, but a greyhound, with its deep chest, thick muscles, and bent spine, still looks ready to race even when at rest. An achievement-oriented person or such a specialist dog is limited and less versatile than a wolf or person who has a more flexible and polymorphous relation to the world, both psychologically and somatically. Many people today are taking this lesson from the wolf and rediscovering their bodies and reintegrating mind and body in the center of their being through such body-awareness activities as yoga, tai-chi, and aikido.

An interesting side note: a gardener, working next door, saw one of my wolves in our yard and, thinking she looked miserable and obviously distressed at being so confined, he complained to me. Once he was out of sight, though, the wolf relaxed and began to play with her companion (a mongrel dog). The gardener, as a strange male presence, made her react this way and changed her entire body language (which he had read correctly). She was distressed and apprehensive — but the gardener was unaware of the context that his presence created: an important observer-interference effect of which those interested in studying animal and human behavior should be aware! She was, in fact, quite content and adapted to her cage and playmate.

Consciously or unconsciously communicated, our body language and demeanor affect other people, wolves, and other animals, sometimes in the same way, but not always. A direct, open stare in man, though threatening

The relaxed stretching of the wolf is a display in itself and may be related to the more exaggerated stretch and bow which is a play-soliciting signal, both of which a man can mimic with his dog (or wolf) and evoke an appropriate response by crossing the "species barrier" through body language.

to a wolf, might be interpreted in one cultural context as rude or assertive, and in another as open, honest, and trustworthy. Similarly, we must be guarded in interpreting what we see in animals as well as in people; our presence, as with the gardener, could affect their behavior and emotions and we may also misinterpret what we see because of our own enculturated or anthropocentric world view. For example, to have a friendly wolf seize your face in its jaws would seem to be flirting with death to an outside observer, but the experience is one of tender control of power in a context of affectionate greeting.

I have described elsewhere at length the various displays and communication signals — vocal, visual, tactile, and olfactory — in the wolf* and have chosen not to repeat that description here but rather have focused on some of the more dynamic and ephemeral aspects of wolf body language. Especially intriguing is the general demeanor of the animal in relation to its situation- or social-context-derived personality, which may change with the situation or context. The wolf displays and then returns to normal equipoise within the constraints of its social rank, which may change subsequently as will its entire demeanor and body language, especially if it comes to assume an alpha or omega position. The same holds true for man, but perhaps man may indeed be less flexible psychically and somatically, particularly since certain displays and attitudes can become "frozen" body habits, such as a permanent stoop of submission or raised shoulders of fear.

* M. W. Fox, *The Behavior of Wolves, Dogs and Related Canids* (New York: Harper & Row, 1971).

By way of summary, the wolf "language" per se serves to increase, decrease, or maintain a certain proximity to another wolf; most of the signals given are intentions (to attack, approach, roll over, flee, chase, etc.). The signals are often mixed, in that two intentions may be successively or simultaneously combined, as a simple form of syntax or sentence structure. A growl and a whine may mean "Keep away, although I like you"; a snarl with lips pulled back submissively may mean "Keep away, even though I know you are my superior." Growl, whine, snarl, and submissive grin can occur in varying degrees of intensity, so that the wolf has a wide communication repertoire at its disposal.

The play bow, somewhat similar to a dog's, is a special signal of "Let's play." It may well be derived from stretching ("I feel relaxed in your presence"). Wolves will often stretch in an exaggerated way in front of a companion and then approach and greet, or assume a deeper, more exaggerated stretch with a clear open-mouthed "play face" and solicit play. Lois Crisler, in her book *Arctic Wild*, noted how her wolves seemed to calm down when she stretched, yawned, and relaxed. Conversely, suddenly tensing and looking in a particular direction will usually make a wolf do the same. With each other, the tendency to do the same thing at the same time is an important aspect of pack coordination and integration. Similarly in man, someone suddenly relaxing in a group can catalyze others to behave in a like manner, as can a depressed, anxious, humorous, or assertive person. Mimicry certainly operates here and this may be the primary key to fellow feeling or empathy. It is also the key to culture, since without the capacity for mimicry and observational learning, little could be transmitted from one generation to the next, other than genetic information.

A wolf also expresses with its entire body such subjective emotional states as joy, pleasure, curiosity, playful humor, anxiety, guilt, and depression. We should not be surprised that wolves feel and experience emotions much as we do, since their social ways are similar to our own ancestral patterns, and the brain centers mediating such reactions are virtually identical in wolf and man.

Wolves and Sympathetic Resonance

Negative expectations and mythos aside, one feels a definite *presence* when with a wolf that is not "blocked" by fear from resonating with you. The wolf's different reactions toward men, women, and children are indicative of a degree of awareness, which is verified further by studies of captive, hand-raised wolves. Females, in the breeding season, may be more assertive and often predictably unpredictable with strange human females. A male wolf may be extremely assertive to men during the breeding season but not toward women, to whom he may be excessively solicitous! Socialization with man, therefore, has some sexual ramifications, since a wolf obviously senses the difference between men and women.

Another aspect of awareness and sympathetic resonance has been afforded by my experiences as a veteri-

Socialized to man from an early age, the wolf will regard its human foster family as its own pack, expressed spontaneously here with the alpha author and his own two cubs, Mike Jr. and Camilla.

narian with sick or injured tame wolves. I have been able to do a number of painful procedures (repeated injections, regularly irrigating infected wounds, etc.) without restraining or muzzling the animal as would have to be done with many dogs. (All that is needed is a gentle hand and reassuring voice, and love and trust *for* the animal.) Of course, with a wild, unsocialized wolf, fear and defensive aggression would be anticipated (yet, curiously, not always forthcoming), but once a wolf is socialized or emotionally bonded, a deep level of trust and obvious understanding is evident.

Because of man's bond with the wolf, the tame wolf responds to man with the same understanding, trust, and affection as it presumably would exhibit in the wild toward its own species. An injured wolf will often be solicitously groomed by a companion and there is one field report of an injured wolf, unable to hunt, being brought food each day by its packmates until it recovered. Such sympathetic resonance — understanding and empathy — provides the basis for altruism and compassion, attributes not necessarily limited to man but perhaps more widespread in the animal kingdom, especially in those species that have complex and cooperative social behavior and organization. An awareness of "self" in relation to "other" must be operating and thus one may wonder about such hypothetical constructs as ego, superego, social modes (such as conscience, guilt, social manipulation, deceit, humor), and the core essence of soul or spirit: are they as exclusively human as we might believe, and if not, then how does this change our regard for and relationship with them? The foundations of many established religions and philosophies and their human-centered values and attitudes may seem threatened, but perhaps they are ready to be more firmly and realistically revised and relaid with the cornerstones of kinship and reverence for all life in their rightful places. A bill of rights for animals is the next major sociopolitical and legal step that must be made if we are to move out of this dark age of ignorant and indifferent anthropocentrism.

Wolf, Ritual,
and the Noble Savage

Rousseau's view of aboriginal man as the "Noble Savage" has some relevance to our cultural perceptions and understanding of wild animals, particularly those such as the wolf who, like man, are hunters. The "Noble Savage" has a certain ineffable mystique, a presence and grace, which, in "civilized" man, can create a yearning to be at one again with nature and to be able to live as a free spirit, without the dependencies that an overcivilized technological world creates.

For Rousseau and other "nature mystics," the archetype of the Noble Savage was a symbol of mankind's oneness with nature, which we, as civilized beings, have almost lost. In this picture of the Noble Savage, we see our own loss of innocence and the yearning to return once again to the lost paradise, the garden of Eden, the Peaceable Kingdom.

Wolf in profile.

By analogy today, the wolf has become the symbolic manifestation of wildness — the archetype of a consciousness of wildness. There is a growing movement in the U.S., for example, to make the wolf the national mammal. The Noble Savage is being replaced by the Noble Wolf, which may be a healthy sign in that we are beginning to see and appreciate animals in their own right and not project ourselves onto them. The very concept of the Noble Savage is surely an idealized, romantic, and egocentric symbol. Yet at the time when this archetype was acceptable, Western man was still too anthropocentrically focused to be able to identify and empathize with a wild animal such as the wolf. It was easier to identify with a wild man than with a wild dog, as it was with the pastoral beauty of the European countryside than with the harsh realities of the wilderness per se (the former was, and still is, no more than an orderly and relatively sterile parkland; only two remnants of original virgin forest are now left in Great Britain, for example).

The American writer Henry Beston clearly spells out our need for a more sensitive and zoocentrically focused view of animals:

We need another and wiser and perhaps a more mystical concept of animals. Remote from universal nature, and living by complicated artifice, man in civilization surveys the creature through the glass of his knowledge and sees thereby a feather magnified and the whole image in distortion. We patronize them for their incompleteness, for their tragic fate of having taken form so far below ourselves. And therein we err, and greatly err. For the animal shall not be measured by man. In a world older and more complete than ours they move finished and complete, gifted with extensions of the senses we have lost or never attained, living by voices we shall never hear. They are not brethren, they are not underlings; they are other nations, caught with ourselves in the net of life and time, fellow prisoners of the splendor and travail of the earth.*

The wolf may well be the modern analog of the Noble Savage archetype for the new renaissance that heralds a growing societal awareness and concern for the protection of the environment and wildlife. It may therefore represent a maturity in our regard for wildness; we can identify more directly with nature without having to resort to an intermediary (in the form of the "savage"), especially once the negative myths about wolves are put to rest as, by analogy, Rousseau *et al.* attempted to put to rest the negative attitudes that prevailed, in their time, toward other races, particularly "primitive" and "savage" and "uncivilized" native people.

There is a curious similarity between the archetypes of the Noble Savage

* *The Outermost House* (New York: Ballantine Books, 1971), p. 67.

and the Noble Wolf as the epitomization of wildness as consciousness; namely, both are highly civilized in terms of social rituals.

Many tribal peoples today have extremely complex rituals and traditions, which we, relatively "rootless" Westerners (especially those of us in the New World who no longer live in ethnic or religious communities), are to a large extent lacking. In a behavioral sense, modern man is becoming increasingly deritualized in many of his behaviors and cultural traditions, ranging from dress fashions to social roles (e.g., the unisex look, women in executive roles). The more cross-cultural mixing that occurs, the more are culture-specific rituals diluted and those (if any) that replace them are transculturally amorphous or polymorphous: less exaggerated, less stereotyped, and more flexible and variable. In addition, modern man is perhaps more adaptable than the Noble Savage in that he can move freely between cultures because of a growing commonality of values (primarily materialistic/economic) as well as a lack of rigid social rituals and taboos.

My comparative studies of wolves and domesticated dogs lead me to speculate that the process of domestication has a similar diluting and simplifying effect on ritualistic aspects of wolf behavior.

The wolf and Noble Savage inspire and enthrall us with their highly evolved social rituals, and we may well ask what has the loss of such ritual done to us, and to our dogs for that matter.

Not having to conform to various rituals (obedience to elders, submission to the leader, displays of allegiance, assertion of rank, etc.), we are "free" in an egalitarian democracy to be ourselves. Yet the "self" is partially defined by our relations to others through clearly defined social relationships, roles, rituals, taboos, etc. The loss of ritual therefore may also be the loss of a sense of self, of "roots" so to speak. Such is the price of freedom, and without the cohesive bonding function of ritual, the very fabric of society may be destroyed. Ritual is the "cement" of both tribe and wolf pack. Without it we have a loose "crowd" of people or a temporary, poorly integrated mob of free-roaming dogs. What socially binding substitutes are there when we loose the bond of shared rituals? A utopian sameness of consumables and a common bond of economic necessity, with the mass hypnosis of television creating a uniformity, but not a unity, of values, attitudes, and aspirations. What follows is a growing sense of a loss of self and of individuality, and alienation. To compensate for this, competitive individualism increases, and society disintegrates. No pack of wolves, or tribe of Noble Savages, can have more than one leader and neither can function where individuals compete instead of cooperate.

When I look at the highly ritualistic way in which wolves greet each other and their leaders, and contrast this with what takes place between dogs, I

Sequence of captive wolves engaging in ritualized aggression where dominant wolf on left jaw-wrestles, muzzle-bites and eventually pins subordinate wolf

am impressed by the "nobility" and "presence" of the wolves' ancient rituals. In contrast, the dogs' rituals are less stereotyped, less clearly defined, *not unlike a young, sexually immature wolf cub*. Neoteny, therefore, or infantilism may be operating in the apparent modification of dog behavior rituals through domestication. Enculturation — the merging of our own diverse human cultures — may be having an analogous effect, neotenizing human behavior even more, by diluting various rituals. Advantages, in spite of alienation and destabilization of societies, could well be a greater flexibility in human attitudes, no longer constricted by prescribed rituals and taboos, and a lesser probability for wars between cultures in the future.

I wonder how the "Noble Savage" of Rousseau might have related to a wolf, compared to a present-day person. Aboriginal man was certainly closer to the wolf and other wild creatures, on a daily basis, than most of us. He

to ground. Neither is injured in this highly ritualized behavior.

would have had a general, pragmatic knowledge of wolves and certainly, as a hunter himself, a deep respect for them. In killing the wolf, many hunting societies had elaborate rituals to give thanks to, or to appease, the wolf's spirit. Yet today, in spite of our great technological advances, we are more ignorant than ever before about wolves and nature itself insofar as only a few scientists, students, and nature lovers are privy to such knowledge. Unlike the Noble Savage we do not need to know about wolves and nature in order to survive. Such knowledge today, for urban man, seems irrelevant if not arcane. We may feel alienated and "rootless" in society with its lack of binding rituals and the horrifying consequences of competitive individualism, and nature may be our last hope for the recovery of sanity and of civilization. And the wolf can be our guide and archetype, more real, indeed, and more relevant, than some illusory Noble Savage.

Wolf, Ritual, and the Noble Savage / 93

When Man Becomes Wolf

When a wolf is socialized to man, it will relate toward man very much as it would to one of its packmates in the wild. Thus, with some captive wolves, care must be taken when a strange person is introduced: he may be rebuffed, as a strange wolf would be in the wild.

Prolonged absence of the "owner" or human leader of the wolf pack might cause complications, too. As in the wild, the loss of the leader would mean a new social order in the pack, with a new leader. If the old leader were to return, he might be rebuffed or conditionally accepted after being subordinated by the new leader or he might, by overcoming the new leader, regain his alpha wolf position. This did happen to one colleague in Holland, who, after an extended field trip, returned to his pack and went into the enclosure to greet them as usual. For-

Unconsciously we communicate in similar ways with animals: we smile in greeting like the wolf and bow low as a friendly gesture.

A wolf pack.

getting the nature of the wolf and the dynamics of the pack, he was surprised when the friendliest male (i.e., the social aspirant of the pack) stood over him in a full threat display!

Although there is not one single authenticated case of a healthy wolf in the wild attacking a man, I was somewhat "privileged" by such an experience with a captive wolf. I crossed the species barrier unwittingly, during the filming of an NBC documentary, *The Wolf Men*, and was attacked by a male wolf as a sexual rival. His mate had taken a liking to me and had displayed her affection in her cage, much to her mate's displeasure (he drove her away and then snarled at me). When released into a large enclosure for filming, he subordinated me and his mate supported him in the attack, but once he was pulled off me, she allowed me to restrain her and was quite passive. These wolves were not mine and I was a stranger to them. More recently, I had a similar experience with captive Iranian wolves and the male remembered me six months later, as did his solicitous mate!

A wolf socialized to man may be dangerous if one is not aware of this wolf law of respecting pair bonds and not getting between them!

Another rule that the male respects is to keep out of the den when the cubs are born. The she-wolf usually will not allow the male into the den for several days. One person who kept wolves was not mindful of this wolf law and entered the enclosure of a she-wolf who had just delivered a litter of cubs. But for the intervention of a friend, the wolf could have killed him. Thus, when one is close to wolves, and vice versa, and when the species barrier is down, one must be aware of and respectful of these wolf rules and rituals. (They are *not* dogs and do not make pets, see pages 121–126.) In such socialized contexts with man, wolves are not vicious, but they are still just wolves and man may come to be regarded as a fellow wolf and must act with due understanding, caution, and respect!

Wolf Communion

I often wish that wolves could actually talk. Then I might know what's going on in their heads: what they are *thinking* about. They do "talk" in an affective, analogical sense, to communicate their emotions and intentions, and they can share certain emotions and expectations. But totally absent in their overt behavioral repertoire is anything comparable to people's sharing of thoughts, ideas, and factual, objective, rational and abstract bits of information. In terms of such mental activity, they seem to have no minds, no capacity to step outside of the present. In the existential and social context of their being, the mental content is primarily bound to the here and now of various stimuli in their environment. Being together and sharing the same experiences is not the same as sharing concepts outside of the immediate context of their exist-

*Communion is easier to
experience than to explain.*

ence. Do they have no mind for this form of mental activity, or are they of
one mind? I opt for the latter. Being of one mind in the existential sense
is a state of being in which the sharing of concepts is not only redundant —
it is impossible, because this aspect of the wolf's mind may not have become
individuated from the collective mind of wolves. Perhaps the psi-trailing
phenomenon described earlier could be explained on the basis of the wolf's
capacity to make contact with its companions beyond the normal range of
its basic senses. A Jungian psychologist calls this the "collective unconscious-
ness" in man. I would hypothesize that it has become relatively unconscious
in us because we are not as existentially grounded in the eternal now as is
the wolf, nor are we so in touch with our feelings, senses, and the external
environment. Also, our preoccupation with "thinking" (and its product —
talking to ourselves or to each other) tends to cut us off from the eternal now
and from our collective and personal subconscious. This part of our minds
that enables us to think abstractly, to objectify, to separate self from context, to bind time and to exchange personal ideas — mental pictures —
verbally, may have its roots in the kind of collective consciousness of the
wolf who may share the same mental pictures with other wolves because in
their "wolfness" they are of one mind. This is not meant to imply that
wolves are not individuals but rather they are less consciously individuated

Wolves howl when alone for pleasure and also to seek contact with companions, and when together, the chorus in the true sense of the word may be a group ritual expressing their unity and kinship through song.

(and separated, even alienated) than we are. It is our verbalizing — image-creating and mental "hologram"-sharing capacity — that separates us from wolves and all other creatures as it may also separate us from our collective and personal conscious (which becomes the "unconscious"). Might it not also separate us from the collective conscious of our animal kin?

Most of the time I believe it does, except in those rare moments when we commune. The other day, while I was reading a book, thinking, and taking notes, one of my wolves came over to me and simply placed her great head on my arm and looked at me. She remained quite still for what seemed an eternity, simply being with me. Just being in the here and now: no overt action or reaction. This is what I believe J. A. Boone, in *Kinship with All Life*, was describing when the dog Stronghart had such a profound impact on his state of mind and perceptions. Such a state of full awareness without action, of pure being in the immediate yet eternal now is one state of consciousness experienced during meditation. Boone felt that Stronghart taught him to meditate. I often meditate with my wolves and this shared state of being, I believe, involves the collective consciousness of all life and that part of our minds which can connect with others when we cease to think, to intellectualize.

In this context, there is no information exchange (of thoughts, ideas, emotional or intentional signals, or expectations). There is simply a deep awareness of being together: barriers between species and between individuals are momentarily transcended. There is no content, in the usual sense of information exchange and processing, for content is replaced by a sense of oneness within the immediacy of a shared moment of being. This is, I feel, the eternal "ground of being" referred to by Buddhist and Taoist philosophers.

What we see, hear, feel, and generally experience through our senses is not always real. Attitudes, conditioned expectations, and habitual modes of thinking and reacting get in the way of the clarity of our perceptions. Consequently, reality is often distorted by the biased ways in which we filter, intepret, and judge things external to us. Some, for example, think that a wolf's eyes display shiftiness, cunning, or evil. Especially when they "light up" at night (when the *tapetum* at the back of the eye reflects one's flashlight, campfire or even the moonlight), the beholder may believe he is seeing the burning fire of a blood-lusting demon from hell. He sees what he believes. Others hear what they believe: more than one trapper has recounted his fear and narrow escape from "certain death" when a pack of wolves was howling in the twilight all around him. As he might interpret the fire in their eyes as evil, so the howl has a dread foreboding in his paranoid misperceptions.

When one can let go of the security of one's beliefs, misconceptions, and unfounded fears, one will discover a wholly new and beautiful world where one's soul touches the spirit essence within all living things. As a man thinks, so is his world. If we can let go and stop imposing our minds upon what we see and feel just for a moment, a remarkable shift in human consciousness occurs. In so doing, one discovers one's own center and a sense of true communion with things external, freed at last from intruding and imposing thoughts and projected feelings.

David Spangler gives a clear picture of this natural state of being, of communion — "a process of attuning to an inner, subjective state of mind which is in resonance with a larger and more impersonal level of consciousness which I may wish to contact. Properly achieving this attunement is largely a matter of holding in the totality of awareness (which includes thought and feeling and spiritual imagination) a sense of what I wish to contact and then relaxing into a sensitive, listening kind of attention. I find my identity blending with the identity of a particular *level* of consciousness and life, not necessarily with a particular being. . . . I remain myself, fully conscious as a human being, yet I become something else as well, in a deep, empathetic relationship out of which information, meaning, insight and teaching can emerge."*

Words are not adequate to describe what is an essentially nonverbal and possibly preverbal state of mind and sharing. The key into such a state of oneness is love, the bond that unites the pack and that can also unite man and wolf, or man and dog or any other sensitive and responsive being. Rationally objective skeptics might contend that I am mystifying the mundane. Indeed, the experience is totally mundane — wholly earthy, grounded and whole in the one reality of the eternal ground of being. The tragedy lies in the fact that such a state of being has become so mystical, so mysteriously alien to us, because we have almost lost contact with this ultimate reality. It is the very ground of our being and the collective consciousness of earth, which has receded outside us (where nature is objectified and living creatures are seen as "things" or unrelated objects) as our collective consciousness has receded inside us into the realm of Freud's unconscious.

In our present mental state of being-in-the-world, we may endeavor to understand, to really "know" animals such as the wolf. But our understanding will be incomplete if we employ only the objective, analytical, intellectual, and abstracting part of our brains. The scientific method developed from this state of consciousness can take us only part way in our search for knowledge, because there is more to reality than bits of factual information. The scientific method can severely limit us when it cuts us

* From *The Findhorn Garden* by The Findhorn Community (New York: Harper and Row, 1975), p. 49.

off from our kinship with all life and from the contingency fields that connect us within the ground of being. We must not abandon the scientific consciousness and method but rather integrate it with the rest of our mental sensing, feeling, and communing being so that we can begin to explore and experience the whole and not a fragment. Without a whole mind, we will never be whole, healthy and in tune with ourselves and with the earth.

Has this objectifying and intellectualizing part of our minds separated us from wolves, nature, and the collective consciousness of all life? I have theorized elsewhere (in *One Earth, One Mind* and *Returning to Eden*) that the evolution of such a mental state may underly our alienation from the natural world and our wholesale, unfeeling exploitation and destruction of other living beings as living "things." Can the earth sustain such a destructive, autonomous, and selfish consciousness? I do not believe that it can. Hence the need for us to expand our minds — to become whole again and to begin to appreciate the wonders and mysteries of life with deep reverence.

Why has one part of our total consciousness evolved and come to dominate our being? Perhaps so that we may objectify, be able to stand outside of context and content and, in so doing, become aware from the outside of our being inside. (Or of the being within the wolf as I have described in this book.) This concept is echoed in the Christian mystic's comtemplative meditation of "God Around and God Within," and the Buddhist, Taoist, and Hindu realization "I am That."

Our evoking minds first became separate from the ground of being as we developed free will, self-awareness, and power over nature. We must now attain self-dominion and reintegrate harmoniously with nature, the eternal ground of being. This is the birth of a new age of consciousness and in the process of our rebirth we must avoid tearing mother earth apart in the process. The wolves, as we, are an inseparable part of mother earth and if we destroy or demean them, we do no less to ourselves. As wolf and man each share the same ground of being physically, so the mind of wolf and man share the same collective consciousness of simply being as well as a vast array of sensations and emotions that are more similar than they are different. And the soul of wolf and man share the same spirit that is in all life: that essence which gives life and which people call creator, God, the light within. The significance of our physical, mental, and spiritual oneness with wolves and all creation has yet to be fully appreciated to the level of changing our thoughts and actions to further the greater good of all life on earth. We have dwelt too much on differences — between races, beliefs, and species — and often only to further selfish interests. Let not the differences between wolf and man continue to be used to demean and exploit the wolf, nor the similarities lead us to an illusory conception of oneness. For it is the otherness of the wolf, the substraction of all that is me within the wolf, that makes it so unique. The wolf, as the "otherness" of me, enriches my life: a world of sameness, of illusory oneness, would be shallow indeed. The telos of the wolf, its "wolfness," is a composite of unique "otherness" and "oneness." Let us appreciate both, and rejoice in the oneness and diversity of all creation, embodied in the soul of the wolf — and of man and earth.

The last lesson from the wolf is "See me not as your enculturated ways and needs dictate, but as I am, for what I am." The wolf is as much a conceptual pattern in our minds as we and wolves are composite patterns of genetically organized, environmentally adapted fields of energy. These lessons from the wolf help us transcend the narrow limits of popular concepts about wolves and nature as a whole, to enlarge out awareness so that more of what is without, is within us also: one earth and one mind, one essence and one spirit. Through nature, through the evolutionary continuum and ecological relatedness and interdependence of all things, we are as much a part of the wolf as the wolf is a part of us. And as we destroy or demean nature, wolves, or any creature, great or small, we do no less to ourselves.

Wolf Kin and Humankind

Wolves and Men

Wolves, like American Indians, lived at peace with nature for thousands of years. Both were hunters, but neither would overkill or hunt for sport. Biologically, and for the Indian also spiritually, these hunters were an integral part of the ecosystem. Prey, such as deer, caribou, and moose, produce excess young, an evolutionary adaptation to anticipated disease and predation. Wolves regulate their numbers, killing off the sick and inferior, and so maintain herd quality and prevent overpopulation and ultimate overgrazing and death from starvation.

To preserve the wolf in captivity, because he is such an intelligent and social animal — perhaps the most highly evolved land mammal in North America — is not enough. The ecosystem of which the wolf is an integral part must also be conserved wherever and whenever possible.

Wolves and Indians were exterminated when they ate the settler's livestock; but there was nothing else to eat since their natural prey had been eradicated to make room for the domestic stock. Indians were given reservations and the interests of white settlers were protected. Wolves need sanctuary and protection from trophy and fur hunters and trappers. In some wolf-free wildlife areas, surplus deer are killed off each year by wildlife management personnel; wolves could be put back in such places in order to restore the ecosystem. They are certainly more appropriate "managers" of deer and have a greater right to hunt than has modern man.

Once, all men supported themselves by hunting, but since modern man has domesticated livestock, hunting is no longer a necessity. It is a sport, a luxury, a service where excess deer must be culled, a crime when predators like wolves and cougars that have never killed farm stock and live miles from human habitation are killed for sport or fur. A crime against nature, because removing such predators upsets the ecological equilibrium and can destroy the ecosystem.

In 1856, the chief of the Duwamish Indians foresaw the white man's demise — "He sees and claims the world for himself and fails to see that he is an integral part of the world."

When modern man can perceive that this is in fact true, he may be able to save the ecosystem of which he is a part but which today he is destroying and making into an impersonal global egosystem. Man is linked with wolf and with all of nature. To break this link is to destroy the spirit of the earth and the essence of humanity within it.

Man, Evolution and Responsibility

Part of the creative genius of *Homo sapiens* is to see the things around him and convert them for his own uses and use them to satisfy his many needs. A rock may be shaped into a flint; a deer is potential food and clothing and fishing lines from skin and sinews; a tree, timber for a house; a river, a source of hydroelectric energy; a wilderness of shale, energy for our cities. As man evolves and explores the world around him, he discovers more that can satisfy and support society and the cancerlike, energy-consuming creations of technology.

The world is seen in terms of one's needs, and a new discovery, a new source of energy, or a faster or more productive machine is a mark of progress. The male ego is fed by values supporting growth, progress, and exploration and operates by controlling, manipulating and exploiting.

The tragic flaw in human perception, though, is that modern man does not really see the world as it really is. It is seen only in terms of how it can satisfy certain needs. "See me for what I am, not as you wish to use me," is the silent cry of wilderness, of wolf, whale, forest, and ocean alike.

Seeing an eagle, a puma, a wolf, or a whale as the thing in itself, no man could kill it without first questioning his own reasons for doing so. In seeing, such a man has matured at last beyond the primitive ego that feels pride and status in hunting and killing. He has matured by establishing a new connection in his brain and by breaking an old one that he inherited from his forefathers. The new connection gives him a greater awareness, which is the key to understanding life for what it is and others for what they are. The old connection tied him to the world, where the world of nature is merely an extension of himself, an egosphere, if you wish. Once broken, he becomes a free man, no longer controlled by or imposing his needs, values, and rights on others, be they wolves or other men. Other people, wolves, and indeed all living things suddenly have rights and intrinsic values in themselves. Their needs can now be seen and understood at last, and are no longer felt as a means or an obstacle to the fulfillment of one's own needs.

Yes, it is the overriding motive of conquest, which is the stamp of modern man as it was of our primitive hunter ancestors. For similar selfish reasons, man will strive to conquer cougar, wolf, deer, women, oceans, mountains, new continents, and even outer space. So preoccupied with such outer diversion, we have hardly begun to explore our "inner space" — the greatest conquest for man is the inner space of his being.

Once a man can see a tree, a wolf, or his fellow and value the other for what it, he, or she is, then his world will be very different. He will rediscover the brotherhood of humanity and reverence for all life, and foster this in others and in his children. Kinship with nature is the key to this awareness. No man can look inward, however, when he is looking at the world through the sights on his gun, which is a world view as narrow and destructive as his egocentric perception and values.

Man, a product of the creative/evolutionary process, now has the potential of this process in his consciousness and actions. He is both a product of creation as he is creator himself. Being so, he is both animal and god: having a biological kinship with all life and a responsibility for all creatures. Consciousness-raising, therefore, implies that mankind must become aware of this responsibility where his own actions or inactions, values and needs, can assist or destroy the evolutionary process. Mankind's destiny and the future of the world is our burden of responsibility and our price for the freedom to be.

Wolf Conservation and Human Salvation

Rid of unfounded fear, prejudice, and the need to gratify ego and pocket by killing, a man will pull up his trap lines and lay down his gun. Such actions are a sign of maturity through understanding nature and appreciating the wolf and all other sentient beings in their own light. Every living thing should surely have equal consideration of its rights to life, freedom, humane treatment, and so forth. But man is slow to mature to this degree of empathetic and ethical awareness and responsibility.*

We have become as alienated from nature as we have from ourselves, our consciousness being geared egocentri-

* For those interested in exploring the question of animal rights in more depth, see R. K. Morris and M. W. Fox, *On the Fifth Day: Animal Rights and Human Ethics* (Washington, D.C.: Acropolis, 1978) and M. W. Fox, *Returning to Eden: Animal Rights and Human Liberation* (New York: Viking, 1980).

Future wolves may all look out onto their former wilderness from the confines of a life in captivity. We must all work to conserve such natural habitat and keep the wolf in designated wilderness sanctuaries as part of our national heritage and obligation as stewards to all life.

cally to competitive individualism. The ecosphere becomes our egosphere to exploit as we choose; man against nature. We kill and destroy, not so much for our own survival per se, but for reasons of pleasure (luxury furs), sport (trophy hunting), and profit and progress. The wolf and its world are as endangered today as is the spirit of humanity, since our fulfillment is in and through nature and not in the artifacts — false gods — of our own making. My concern, therefore, is not solely for conservation and the future of endangered species but also over the state of human consciousness — those needs, attitudes, and values which threaten the survival of all species, including man.

Appreciation of the wolf — of the thing in itself, independent of its relationship, if any, with human needs — can be a first step in freeing human consciousness from its imprisoned egocentric and self-destructive world view. Understanding the wolf with fellow feeling, respecting its intrinsic right to live independent of the "right" of sports hunters who want the moose, caribou, and deer all for themselves, and valuing the role of the wolf as part of the natural wilderness ecosystem are all positive

Wolves were once widespread throughout most of the U.S. Most have been exterminated, like these coyotes, by ranchers using poison bait and also by hunters and trappers. It is too late for man to live harmoniously with nature when there is nothing left.

A pair of coyotelike red wolves. This race lives in Texas and Louisiana and is endangered.

attitudes gained with a heightened, more mature consciousness. Such awareness for man is our key to liberation from the global neurosis of egocentricity and dominionistic utility. Giving the wolf sanctuary will help human sanity; as a result, conservation becomes an act of consciousness-raising. Nature reflects the inner state of the human psyche. The more chaotic, disrupted, defiled, depleted, and polluted becomes the natural ecosystem, the more apparent becomes the disorder of our own lives and society.

Conservation is an affirmation of being a responsible human being, since our survival and fulfillment depend upon it. We are not conserving our "resources" (a common valuation for things of nature) but insuring our own future, our physical and psychic health, since as a man thinks and acts, so becomes his world.

These lessons from the wolf can help change human consciousness, and indeed a radical mutation in attitudes and values is needed if we are going to conserve what little is left of nature, and if we are to survive ourselves.

We can justify saving the wolf or *any* sentient being on three levels. First and hightest, on aesthetic, empathetic, and ethical grounds; second, economic, since it is important to maintain the rich diversity of nature for future generations; third, survival per se, since further depredation, destruction, and pollution of the biosphere could set off chain reactions that would make our overpopulated planet unlivable. Few people are at the first level, since immediate short-term economic motives justify exploitation and depletion of natural resources and extinction of species. The second level is often confused with the third — survival; many believe that it is essential for our survival to strip-mine and further destroy natural ecosystems in many other ways. But we do not need to be so destructive since our survival is not yet at stake although it soon may be if the rate of entropy continues without checks and alternatives. It is the survival of outmoded institutions and values — progress, profit, and unlimited growth — that is at stake and that we confuse with self-survival. For a dependent member of a wholly materialistic society, this may be true, if he identifies his life wholly with that social system's values and goals and can see no alternatives.

There *are* alternatives and we must discover them in a new set of values and responsible ethics based upon a reverence for all life.* It is in this way that the conservation of the wolf and the future of man, his very salvation, are inextricably bound, for the factors which endanger the wolf threaten mankind's future as well.

* See M. W. Fox, *One Earth, One Mind* (New York: Coward, McCann and Geoghegan, 1980).

Evolution: Wolf and Man

Millennia ago, in the Pleistocene era, wolf and man evolved and were both hunters, but man continued to evolve. Whereas the wolf became adapted and "at one" with its environment, man continued to change himself by changing his environment. His creative curiosity and use of symbols (words, art forms, and tools, which were the material expression of values and ideas) as a means of nongenetic transmission of information set him apart from nature and other species. He was evolving increasingly under his own direction and for better or for worse; new symbols and ideas acted in the same way, but infinitely more rapidly, as new gene combinations do for other animals. Unlike an animal that has to wait generations for a genetic transformation to change its actions, evolutionary direction, and ability to adapt to new environmental niches, man can

Iranian wolf. This is the smallest of the various races of wolves. This Asiatic race is thought by many to be the principal ancestor of the domesticated dog.

effect the same transformations consciously, by acquiring new values and perceptions, and technology is the physical manifestation of these mental genes or "mnemes." Such transformations can be instantaneous and thus we became increasingly self-determining, freed from genetic and environmental constraints. This is essentially how man became "unstuck" from the tapestry of patterned organization in nature. Why — and for what purpose — we do not know unless one believes that man, "created in the image of God," is to become god or co-creator himself. Such a preordained destiny, as proposed by the Jesuit philosopher Teilhard de Chardin, is not illogical* considering the pattern in which life unfolds toward increasing complexity, consciousness, integration, and synthesis.

When man became "unstuck" from nature, he began crudely (and crudely still today, although crises and errors are beginning to direct and reshape his consciousness and actions) to take nature into himself creatively. He began to domesticate plants and animals and, in so doing, started to learn to be creator in his own right. He was a utilitarian domesticator. Now he is learning slowly to become a steward and a co-creator with nature. He is becoming the weaver of his own cosmic dreams and through

* See M. W. Fox, *One Earth, One Mind* (New York: Coward, McCann and Geoghegan, 1980).

him, in consciousness, nature is manifesting gradually its ultimate fulfillment. Historically, as well as today, mankind has abused this creative freedom, within which are the fruits of his fulfillment as well as the seeds of his own personal and global destruction. The state of the human mind determines the state and future of the world and we must attain dominion over our own minds if we are to succeed in accomplishing our evolutionary potential — if not ultimate purpose and destiny.

Conclusions

A few people are fortunate enough to meet someone — perhaps a teacher, or an artist, philosopher, or man of science or letters — who adds something to their lives for which they remain eternally grateful. It may be insight, depth, direction, inspiration, faith, courage, purpose, or meaning: one or many qualities, some ineffable, even mystical or spiritual, others profoundly simple or practical, that add to the sum total of one's existence, a significance precious beyond measure. For other people it may be some experience or natural event, like climbing a mountain, being alone in the wilderness or lost in a snowstorm, contemplating a beautiful sunset, or observing the birth of an animal or the death of a loved one.

These two modes — the first, *relationship* with another person, the second *experience* of (or communing with) some natural phenomenon — comprise the essence of life: experiencing and relating, communion and communication. The intuitive and the rational, the subjective and the objective, the emotional and the intellectual are all seemingly opposite yet complementary states in which one's awareness (through experiencing and relating with other things, events or persons) is enhanced and enriched.

For me, there has been no single person, no great teacher or man of words or actions; there has been no single natural place or event that has meant more or less to me than what the wolf, in the totality of its being and presence, has shared with me. Some may react with critical scorn, interpreting this as a morbid or bizarre lupomorphic fixation or an anthropomorphic projection, contending that only the world of man and the words and actions of esteemed teachers are significant and real. All else is a figment of subjective imaginings. But the wolf became my teacher, my source of inspiration, reflection, and understanding. Many nature mystics, Zen-oriented philosophers, and more subjectively intuitive and empathetically balanced "objective" scientists and humanists alike find sympathetic resonance with things in and of nature. There are many lessons from nature, unexplored, unwritten, and untold volumes in fact, that contain all the mysteries, truth, and ultimate significance of life.

Animals, embodying, incorporating, and manifesting these myriad lessons from nature, can make us more human. By this, I mean that nature and animals can help us know why we are, what we are, and at the same time deepen our awareness, appreciation, and sensitivity toward all life. Such understanding leads us toward a fuller expression of being human — living responsibly and with compassionate reverence for all life.

Centering and Grounding

When we really begin to understand the nature of man and animal, we do not essentially have a greater ability to communicate (or control or manipulate). Rather, the awareness of the essence of life manifest in all sentient beings leads to a new and deeper mode of relatedness: empathetic communion, which, in many instances can be and is directly reciprocated. One must first be centered in one's own essence of being, neither blocked objectively or lost subjectively with a set of ideas, attitudes, expectations, and the like. Such centering, which is the key of one's inner world to the outer world — is the key to the kingdom between animal and man.

Wolves helped me discover my own center. A wolf, like any wild creature, is both totally centered in the inner reality of its being and grounded in the "eternal now" of its relatedness to external reality. Wolves lead me from the far-off center of my initial objective involvement as a curious scientist, to the subjective realm of affection and attachment toward those animals that I raised from cubs and for whom I became both foster parent and pack leader.

One might question how "real" a wild animal like a wolf is when it is raised in captivity. In one or two generations a wolf will not lose its wildness; it is not domesticated but is, instead, "tame," still retaining its wild potentials. Its fear of man, however, has been eliminated and replaced with trust, love, and understanding. It is only when such fear is removed that man and animal (and man and man for that matter) may communicate, relate, share, and also commune. Fear, in man and animal alike, is associated negative attitudes — prejudice, catastrophic expectations, and such — that block sympathetic resonance, affection, love, empathy, and understanding.

What, then, when fear is absent and such rapport is established: how "real" is it and how much of what is experienced is merely a figment of human imagination lost in subjective anthropomorphic projections or zoomorphic introjections? Here, objectivity is essential, allowing rational, reflective detachment and appraisal of the subjective experience co-simultaneously: this is "centering" and at the same time one is also "grounded" in the reality of an eternal moment of relatedness. Such "grounding" in the here and now is what one commonly experiences and associates with animals and children, who are in contact with the reality of the here and now and are not lost in *thinking*. Thinking about what one is going to do or to experience, or what might or might not happen, or what one should or should not do interferes with perceiving (sensing) and acting (or responding) spontaneously. Openness, sensitivity, authenticity, and receptivity are then greatly limited by attachment to thoughts and preoccupation with analyzing. Two common bases for this self-limiting mode of interacting are ingrained *habit* and *fear*.

In this kind of grounding in and through relatedness, all thinking and anticipating on the basis of prior negative experiences, fear, conditioned expectations, and so on, is stilled. One simply *is* relating without thinking/doing, relating spontaneously, in what I call a pure state of "being-awareness." Grounding, therefore, is the same as centering, the latter being an integrated state when one is alone and the former an integrating state when one is in some social context.

One West Coast psychiatrist who had some friendly wolves used them "therapeutically" with emotionally disturbed adolescents, realizing perhaps intuitively the very positive grounding and centering effect such animals can have on a person. (Similarly, domestic dogs are being used today as "cotherapists" to help both disturbed children and adult patients.)

We can not only learn to appreciate something of the wolf and the nature of wildness from these lessons from the wolf, but also gain some insights into our own nature as well.

Many people who have been with my wolves, even if only for a few moments, come away feeling "refreshed," "like having had a super shower," "cleansed," "real and alive." Such remarks, I think, dramatically describe and confirm what I have been describing as lucidly as possible. Clarity of vision and clarity of feeling are one, but since the latter is often so highly subjective and personal, I feel that I must confine myself as much as possible to stating objectively in this book what I have learned from the wolves, and not indulging in subjective emotional descriptions. This way, I hope, the lessons from the wolf have the clarity and directness for you, through me, as they had for me directly from the wolf. Even so, Konrad Lorenz, at the opening reception of an international conference on ethology, shocked some "objective" scientists present by stating with characteristic zeal that "you must first love your animal before you can study it."

I would rather rephrase this by saying, "You must first love your animal before you can learn from it," and by love, both Lorenz and I mean openness, sensitivity, and empathy, which is the key to intuition, clarity of vision, and understanding. It is therefore the key to our humanness, and in these lessons from the wolf I hope that I have helped increase our love and appreciation, not only for wolves, but for all creatures great and small.

Postscript

After reading this book you may want to get a wolf cub and raise it as a pet or even breed wolves in captivity. They are certainly easy to purchase from zoos and wild "pet" ranches, but I strongly advise against this. Wolves do *not* make pets and no matter how experienced with animals you may be, you won't be helping wolves by keeping one or breeding them in captivity. I, like many, have learned this lesson myself, although my having wolves was not for pet pleasure but for behavior research.

Please read this memorandum written by one of my colleagues, the late Dr. Douglas Pimlott, who may more firmly convince you not to keep a wolf than I have been able to do.

The author with wolf a few years ago on a local TV talk show; in spite of the obvious friendly submissive display of the young wolf, the host keeps a safe distance away and a closed (protective) posture!

Memorandum to: PEOPLE INTERESTED IN KEEPING WOLVES AS PETS
From: Douglas Pimlott

"... I became convinced that the only way to work with captive wolves is to have them from the time they are very young pups. Then, as they grow up, you gain a deep insight into the personality and behaviour of each individual. Confidence in working with animals is based on such understanding and is vital if one is ever to work successfully with wild animals in captivity. I have often wondered if my inability to make friends with Yukon (one of the captive wolves) was not as much my fault as his. I found it difficult to be completely confident when there were no barriers between us. It is possible that this may have been the critical flaw in our relationship.

"But this too is one of the reasons why wolves should not be considered as conventional pets. Under such circumstances they are constantly required to cope with people who do not understand them and who fear them. This compounds the problem and places them in many difficult situations that wolves should not be expected to face.

"Wolves are wild animals. When they are tamed and kept in captivity they should be handled in very special ways. They should have the advantage of facilities that will permit them to have lives of their own, to be wolves and not dogs. I do not mean that they should not have close relationships with people; but such relationships should be restricted to the few who have a real understanding of the animal that is a wolf."

These words appeared in *The World of the Wolf*, a book on wolves which was written by Russell Rutter and me. They appear at the end of the chapter *Wolves as Individuals* in which I had recounted some of the experiences my family and I had in raising wolf pups. I wrote them in spite of the fact that I had also said that our lives had been enriched by a wealth of experience and emotions during the time we had lived or worked with wolves.

Since that time I have received a great many letters from people who want to keep wolves as pets. Some of those who write had read *The World of the Wolf* but were certain that they were the right person to raise a wolf. In some cases they wanted me to help them obtain a wolf or to help them obtain the permit to keep a wolf, which is required in some provinces or states. I am much more convinced now that it is not a wise thing to keep wolves or other large mammals, as pets. I intend to do all I can to promote the enactment of legislation in Canada that will make it illegal to do so. It follows, of course, that I will not do anything to help any person to obtain a wolf as a pet or as a show animal.

I do not argue against keeping wolves in adequate situations in well-managed zoos or game farms. But I stress "adequate situations." I do not consider that they should be kept in small pens, cages, on chains or as lone animals. The reasons I feel the way I do about keeping wolves as pets are complex. Some of my reasoning goes like this:

(1) Wolves are very social animals. Without the social existence that they experience as member of a pack, they tend to be disembodied entities. Because

of this, I consider that when in captivity, they should be provided with areas that are large enough to permit the existence of a pack — a social entity.

Individuals who aspire to keep them as pets can rarely provide the facility that is necessary, nor can many people adjust to the trauma of the intense interactions that occur between wolves under the stress of a captive situation.

(2) Each wolf is an individual, a distinct personality. They cannot be stereotyped and there is no way of assuring that the wolf one obtains will adapt in a "satisfactory" way either to people or to captivity. In *The World of the Wolf* we brought out the great range in personalities that existed in a single litter; two in the litter were highly adaptable, two were marginal, and one would have been very difficult to keep as a personal pet.

(3) I consider that keeping wolves as personal pets is much more likely to harm the cause of wolves than it is to help it. Word of incidents, in which a wolf bites a person, usually spread like wildfire and can nullify a great deal of work to develop a more positive appreciation and understanding of wolves. If a person, particularly a child, was ever killed in North America, it would be a disaster, in terms of wolf conservation.

Further, I consider the efforts to promote the conservation of wolves will be much more effective, over the long term, if they are based on developing an appreciation of wolves as wild animals than if they are based on efforts to prove that wolves are "good guys" by exposing people to captive, semi-domesticated animals.

I believe people are beginning to realize that wolves add an important element of diversity to the world we live in and have an inherent, intrinsic right to share the world with us. In my opinion, these are things we should concentrate on in our efforts to conserve wolves throughout the world.

(4) Finally, I am concerned about the way people react to wolves. Their owners frequently seem to lose all sense of objectivity in dealing with them. They tend to develop the feeling that "their wolf" personifies all good. They cannot seem to remember that the animal they love so much has instincts which developed under natural evolutionary forces not under human control as in the case of dogs. The result is that they frequently do stupid things in showing off their wolf, or wolves, to the public.

Then there are the reactions of people who meet wolves for the first time in a captive situation. The way wolves greet a new acquaintance can be very disturbing to a stranger. In other words, their greeting behaviour can be very rough and is easily misinterpreted by a person who has not had experience with wolves. Serious problems could develop if people run away or show intense fear in such situations.

These are some of my reasons for arguing against wolves as personal pets. If you would like to gain more insight I suggest that you try to obtain copies of two books, *Arctic Wild* and *Captive Wild*, which were written by Lois Crisler. They recount experiences the Crislers had in raising wolves to use in a Disney movie, *Arctic Wilderness*, and then in bringing the wolves back to civilization. *Captive Wild* is of particular interest in terms of keeping wolves is captivity.

Lone wolf howling.

I hope you will understand why I do not feel that I can do anything to encourage or to help any person to obtain a wolf pet.

You can help wolves by joining local and national humane and conservation organizations, a list of which has been included at the end of the book. It is their world that has to be saved: wolves in the wild are endangered, like everything else, and keeping some in cages isn't going to change human values and priorities nor the technopolitics of habitat destruction. You can also help by always being on the alert to inhumane or ecologically and ethically unsound practices, both locally and nationally. Fight for more state wilderness refuges; boycott stores that sell wild caught furs and nations that violate conservation laws or exploit wild animals unnecessarily (like the U.S.S.R. and Japan, who still insist on unlimited whaling); oppose habitat destruction under the guise of recreational development. Subscribe to conservationist magazines. Become familiar with those problem areas that deal with the critical interphase between man, animals, and the environment. You will learn what you can do and choose what you would most like to do (there is so much) as a responsible public citizen with a conscience and influence. Few will ostracize you; most are indifferent or ignorant and just need *you* to wake them up. Schoolchildren can also get involved in this whole-earth education and action (if they haven't done so and reached you already!).

Some may argue: Why waste time, effort, and money on animals? — it's people who need help. Certainly, personal priorities influence one's choice of direction, but for me, helping animals is one of the many indirect ways we can help people to become more humane, compassionate in their actions and ethical in their beliefs. The humane movement is thus one facet of a worldwide, accelerating change in human consciousness — the natural mind of man becoming more at one with the natural world in which lies our ultimate fulfillment and the deepest personal significance in life.

To be kind to animals means to be human: to express one's concern and reverence for all life is the ultimate act of responsible compassion for man. In this way, those in need — animal and man alike — can help us become more human by evoking humane concern and action. To be indifferent to or to exploit others and to act unthinkingly out of habit and without compassion or understanding and empathy is to be less than human. Also when we demean nature — or any embodiment of creation — we demean ourselves. By expressing our humanness through kindness and concern for the lives of all creatures and dedicating our lives to their conservation and welfare, we become more fully human, and our efforts will insure the continuing fulfillment of future generations of our kind and animal kin alike.

Appendix I:
Wolf Fact Sheets

Wolves, Dogs and Other Canids

The family *Canidae* consists of two main subgroups, the vulpines (foxes) and the canines (wolves, coyotes, jackals, and dogs), and some intermediate "fox-dog" forms from South America. Only the latter canines will interbreed. Dogs have been domesticated for over ten thousand years and probably were developed from a dingolike dog, which in various places and at various times was crossbred with indigenous wild species such as wolves and coyotes. Wolves and coyotes have to be superintelligent to survive, and hunting and trapping by man insured that only the quickest to learn and the wisest would survive.

Wolf cubs that have been hand-raised are difficult to train, in contrast to the average dog. Trainability is more related to dependence than to intelligence per se, and one major trait of most breeds of domestic dog is a high degree of dependence. Wolves do *not* make good pets, not only because of this but also because they are extremely inquisitive and destructive. They will excavate a sofa to track down a mysterious smell or squeaky spring in the stuffing!

Of the canid family, the wolf is one of the most social species, since it is a pack hunter. The African Cape hunting dog and the dhole of Southeast Asia are the only other pack-hunting species. Coyotes and jackals occasionally form temporary "packs," which invariably consist of parents and mature offspring and domesticated dogs may turn feral and form small packs. Other canids, especially the foxes, are usually solitary throughout the year except during the breeding season.

Hunting

Wolves will hunt alone, seeking small prey (rodents and rabbits) and picking up what carrion they can. But it takes two or more to bring down larger prey, and by cooperating as a pack they can overcome prey many times their own size. A healthy moose could kill a wolf with its front hooves and a caribou easily outruns any wolf. The wolf pack "tests" the prey to see if it is sick or injured, since they have little chance of catching a healthy one. Wolves will use strategy while hunting, notably driving into an ambush and distracting the prey so that one wolf can rush in safely and get a firm hold. Deer fawns and moose and caribou calves also fall pery to the wolves. This seems cruel, but usually there is a surplus of fawns each springtime (an adaptive "anticipation" of predation), so the population can withstand this and also benefit from the "pruning." Since the calves are all born around the same time and mature quickly, the period when they are vulnerable is very short. In contrast to the wolf, man the hunter, if he has a choice, will not kill the sick and injured but will go for the prime and trophy animals instead. This has a very different effect on the herd and could be detrimental. The wolf has little choice — he must take what he can get — and this is invariably not deterimental to the prey species but is, in fact, beneficial. If it was detrimental, there would be no deer, caribou, or moose left, since wolves have been hunting them for hundreds of thousands of years!

Pack Social Organization

A wolf pack is essentially an extended family consisting of the offspring of a mated pair, one or more juveniles from the previous year, and other nonbreeding adults that are often related to the mated pair and assist them in caring for the young.

Within a pack of six to twelve or more wolves there is a dominance hierarchy, or pack order, that changes as wolves mature, age, and die. There is an alpha or number-one female who dominates the other females and an alpha male who not only rules over the males but is the leader of the pack. He is the decision-maker. Other wolves, even older ones, respond to him submissively and affectionately, as would cubs to their parents. Allegiance to the leader helps keep the pack together and this, together with avoidance of strange wolves and defense of their range against intruders, keeps wolf packs apart. Each pack has its own territory, which is marked out by urinal "scent posts"; occupancy is perhaps advertised by howling.

Body Language

Wolves have a rich vocabulary of visual signals that communicate social rank, mood, and intentions. Subtle changes in tail and ear positions, of body and head angle and height, making and breaking eye contact, and various facial expressions convey this information. Even two emotions of varying intensity, such as fear and submission, or submission and defensive threat, can be signaled at the same time. Although these displays are instinctive, a wolf learns who is who in the pack and what to expect in certain social situations. He is aware of the various roles he and other wolves play in different contexts. This awareness is termed *"metacommunication"* — "He knows that you know that he knows." Because of this, the frequency and complexity of communication signaling can be reduced; a mere glance or slight flick of the ears suffices.

Aggression

Since each wolf knows its place in the rank order, conflicts are reduced. Once a stable dominance hierarchy is established, peace reigns in the pack. Any disagreements are settled by *ritualized fighting* or "jaw wrestling," and sometimes just by a threat display without any physical contact at all. The alpha wolves may "police" others, subordinating an up-start with a direct stare and breaking up squabbles between two lower-ranking wolves.

What seems to be very aggressive is the pinning of whining subordinates to the ground by the growling leader. Subordinates often solicit this; such behavior is not aggressive but is a ritual display of rank between pack members, serving to reaffirm the unity of the pack and allegiance to the leader.

More severe fighting does occasionally break out during the breeding season, and leadership roles may change. A pack may split up at this time. Severe injuries are rare. As soon as a wolf gives a surrender signal and shows submission toward the other con-testant, the latter will immediately stop fighting. Wolves do show chivalry!

Play

Wolves of all ages, from four weeks of age and on, engage in play. They are by nature curious creatures, and any novel item that catches their fancy could become a play object: a stick, piece of antler, or the tail of another wolf. Wolf cubs especially engage in a form of "hallucinatory" self-play, pawing, snapping at, and even chasing their own tails or spooking and pouncing on or running away from nothing, just like a kitten. A stick or strip of deer hide can be a toy for solitary play to be stalked, attacked, shaken, and "killed" or a catalyst for social play even for adult wolves. Suitable objects can be used for tugs of war, chase and catch or even as a "dare," where one wolf dares another to steal its toy.

Then there is the social play of wolves, enjoyed by all pack members. Social play takes many forms. Hugging and wrestling are forms of contact-play which are usually preceded by a "let's play" bow and are especially evident during courtship. Contact play is often interspersed with brief bouts of affectionate grooming and may lead to playful fighting, chasing, stalking, and ambush, involving two, three, and more wolves.

Sex

The bonds that keep a wolf pack together are social, not sexual. A mature female is sexually receptive for only about four to eight weeks in the year. Usually only the alpha female mates. If a low-ranking female attempts to mate with a male, she will usually be blocked by the alpha female. Similarly, a low-ranking male will be inhibited by a male of higher rank. The pack order serves then as a social form of birth control.

Unlike most canids, which reach sexual maturity at one year of age, the wolf is not mature until at least its second year. This *may* be adaptive in keeping the pack together so that yearlings stay with the parents an additional year and help in hunts and in raising young.

Parental Behavior

Much of the social life of the pack revolves around the care and rearing of young. The father brings food to the mother while the cubs are nursing. He carries it in his stomach and regurgitates it at the entrance to the den. When the cubs are older, both parents and other pack members feed them in this way. When parents go off hunting, another adult will baby-sit. Adults play for hours with the cubs and are extremely tolerant and affection-ate, but not overpermissive. Cubs soon learn their places within the pack. Little is known about how the older wolves teach cubs to hunt, but much is probably picked up by ob-servation and imitation alone.

Socialization and Group Rituals

As the cubs play and interact with each other and with adults, they become socialized or emotionally bonded at an early age. This bonding period wanes around four months and cubs begin to shy away from strangers.

Older cubs persist in mobbing the leader, licking his face, whining and tail-wagging in the same way they once did in order to solicit food from their parents. The food-soliciting and mobbing greeting toward parents become the collective "love-in" display of affection and allegiance shown by subordinate adults to the leader. Such ritual ceremonies are performed especially when wolves wake up, before they split up to hunt, and when the pack is reunited after a hunt.

Another ritual often follows this, namely the pack howl or chorus. The sound of a wolf pack in full song perhaps best exemplifies the highly evolved sociability of the wolf.

Appendix II:
Organizations for Your
Support and Involvement

There are many humane and conservation organizations, some with slightly different approaches or specializations from others. This short list will give you some to check out for your own particular interests. Remember, too, at the local level there may be chapter divisions of these national organizations, as well as local groups in conservation, natural history, environmental protection, and animal welfare.

The Alaska Wildlife Alliance, P.O. Box 190953 Anchorage, Alaska 99519.
Fauna Preservation Society, Zoological Society of London, Regents Park, London, England.
The Humane Society of the United States, 2100 L Street, NW, Washington, D.C. 20037.

For those interested in practical, philosophical and legal aspects of animal protection and conservation, see M.W. Fox, *Inhumane Society: The American Way of Exploiting Animals*, St. Martin's Press NY 1990, and for younger readers see M.W. Fox, *Animals Have Rights Too* Crossroad/Continuum N.Y. 1991.